A

MANUAL OF BEE-KEEPING.

BY

JOHN HUNTER,

LATE HONORARY SECRETARY OF THE BRITISH BEE-KEEPERS' ASSOCIATION.

"Some have taught
That Bees have portions of ethereal thought,
Endued with particles of heavenly fires,
For God the whole created mass inspires."—VIRGIL.

𝔗𝔥𝔦𝔯𝔡 𝔈𝔡𝔦𝔱𝔦𝔬𝔫,
THOROUGHLY REVISED AND MUCH ENLARGED.

𝔏𝔬𝔫𝔡𝔬𝔫:
DAVID BOGUE,
3, ST. MARTIN'S PLACE, TRAFALGAR SQUARE.
1879.

PREFACE TO THE THIRD EDITION.

In my position as Honorary Secretary of the British Bee-keepers' Association, I was frequently asked to recommend a moderately priced book, which would instruct the inquirer how properly to manage his Bees; to my great regret I was unable to give a satisfactory reply, being acquainted with no work embracing the requisites of cheapness and completeness up to our then standard of knowledge, to bring it within the means of the many. The best work in the English language was unquestionably 'Langstroth on the Honey Bee'; but this, published in America, costs here ten shillings and sixpence. All others that I knew did not explain the various systems and apparatus sufficiently, or were too costly for general use. It was universally acknowledged that the Apiarian Exhibition of 1874 had given an immense impetus to Bee-culture, and I had great hopes that one of our clever and learned Bee-masters would have announced during the following Winter a new Work on the subject, which would fulfil the desired conditions; but the 1st day of February, 1875, arrived, and I had not heard the wished-for news; so, reluctant to let the Spring appear without the needed help, I resolved, *faute de mieux*, to attempt the work myself; and, having sought and found a publisher, began and completed the First Edition of this little Manual in my leisure evening hours of the same month of February.

The Second Edition followed the first so rapidly that very little enlargement or correction was requisite, but between the publication of the Second Edition to the present time a lapse of three years has occurred, during which time Apiculture has made such rapid strides that the necessity has arisen to thoroughly revise the whole. work, and, in addition, bring prominently before Bee-culturists the modern introduction and use of sectional supers and comb foundation, which jointly will, if I mistake not, revolutionize the art of honey raising in Great Britain, as it has already done in America. Until the British Bee-keeper is awake to the necessity of sending his honey to market in the best saleable form, he cannot hope to compete with our enterprising friends across the Atlantic, who are at this present time invading the honey markets of Europe with the same bold energy they have shown with other crops.

In the preparation of this Volume my aim has been to give the best possible information on the subject it was in my power to obtain, and, without attempting to rely solely on my own personal knowledge, I have gleaned materials for the work from every available source. I have been particularly indebted in this way to 'Langstroth on the Honey Bee,' the various 'Bee Journals' of America and Europe, the articles of Mr. Cheshire in 'The Country,' 'The Journal of Horticulture,' 'King's Bee-keepers' Text Book,' and 'Neighbour's Apiary.' I have, I believe, in most cases acknowledged the author from whom I have borrowed. If, in any instance, this is omitted, it is unintentionally; therefore I hope to be pardoned. My aim has been to make known the various new inventions and appliances in Apiculture, and to encourage the culture of the Bee, by showing what wealth is lost to the nation at large by its neglect, and to give, in a popular and handy form, practical instructions to the novice which may start him fairly on the road to profitable Bee-keeping in a merciful and rational manner. Is it too presumptuous to hope, also, that the adept may herein find some useful hints and facts with which he was not acquainted? Earnestly trusting that my work may not be in vain,

I am, &c.,

JOHN HUNTER.

5, Eaton Rise,
Ealing, Middlesex.
May, 1879.

CONTENTS.

———◆———

CONTENTS.

A MANUAL OF BEE-KEEPING.

NATURAL HISTORY OF THE HONEY BEE.

" What atom forms of insect life appear !
And who can follow Nature's pencil here?"—MRS. BARBAULD.

FROM the very earliest historic times, the Hive Bee has been cultivated by man for the sake of the delicious honey and useful wax that it produces, as well as studied for the manifold lessons it furnishes in industry and physiology.

The busy merchant, when wanting a symbol for his house, could find no better sign than the "Bee-hive." How common the axiom, "A very Hive of industry." The poet and the moralist fails not to quote our little friend as an example to the young; and the beautiful hymn of Dr. Watts, 'The Little Busy Bee,' can never be forgotten as a memory of our early days, and in ages to come will be taught to our children's children with the same loving wish of a good result as was hoped for us.

To the naturalist and man of science, the Bee affords a never-ending store of Nature's wonders; although philosophers, from Aristomachus, four centuries before the Christian era, Cicero, Pliny, Philiscus, Virgil, Theophrastes, Plutarch, and Columella, to those of modern times, Maraldi, Réaumur, Sir Christopher Wren, the illustrious blind Huber, and Lord Brougham, all wrote upon and studied the Bee, the wonders it unfolds are not yet exhausted.

The patience and sagacity of the naturalist have had an ample field for exercise in the study of the structure, physiology, and domestic economy of Bees; their preservation and increase have been objects of assiduous care to the agriculturist; and their reputed perfection of policy and government have long been the theme of admiration, and supplied copious materials for argument and allusion to the poet and the moralist of every age. The accurate investigation of life within a Bee-hive has, from the old form of the latter's construction, been beset with so many difficulties that very often wrong deductions have been drawn from supposed facts discovered, and succeeding authors without confirmation have unwittingly promulgated errors, until much of the written history had become little better than fable, the correction of which is left to our own time and daily improving means of observation.

In Great Britain and on the Continent of Europe there is cultivated, so far as I know, but one species of Hive Bee, although of this there are several varieties. Our common English, or Black Bee, has been scientifically named *Apis Mellifica;* and the Italian, or Ligurian Bee, *Apis Ligustica;* but all entomologists agree that they are one and the same species.

Dr. Gerstacker even goes so far as to consider the Egyptian Bee, *Apis Fasciata,* and another African Bee, *Apis Adansonii,* as varieties also. The best authorities are in a difficulty as to which Bee should rank as the species—whether to say *Apis Mellifica var-Ligustica* or *vice versa.* The former, I think, is the more generally adopted; but our distinguished hymenopterist, Mr. Frederick Smith, late of the British Museum, seemed to consider the most highly coloured as the typical form ; and it is possibly more correct to give the precedence to *Apis Ligustica*, but it cannot be decided satisfactorily until we know in what country the Hive Bee really originated.

Physiologically I can detect no difference between Ligurians and Black Bees. Individuals vary in size as well as in colour; but, on dissecting a number of each variety, the difference is nil, and no microscopist could separate a series of any given organs of both, if mixed indiscriminately. Some observers have asserted that the tongue of the Ligurian Bee is considerably longer than our British native Bee, by which means it is enabled to reach the nectar in the red clover, which its ally cannot do; but I have carefully measured with the micrometer a great many of both varieties, and I do not find more than the one hundredth of an inch difference in favour of the Ligurian, so small a difference being probably attributable to mere accident of breeding.

The leading feature in the natural history of Bees, and one which distinguishes them from almost all other insects, is their singular distribution into three different kinds, constituting to all appearance so many different modifications of sex.

A hive of Bees in June consists of a Queen, Workers, and Drones.

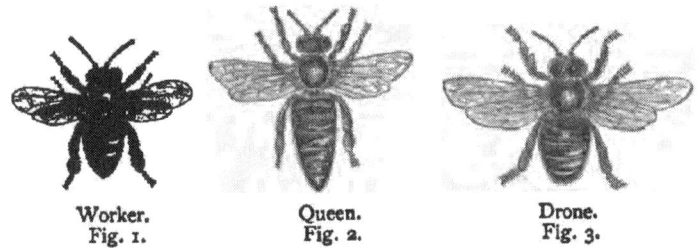

Worker.
Fig. 1.

Queen.
Fig. 2.

Drone.
Fig. 3.

The first (in abnormal circumstances), and at certain

seasons the last, may be absent ; the second never.   The
Queen is the only *perfect* female.

> " First of the throng and foremost of the whole,
> One stands confest the Sovereign and the soul."—VIRGIL.

If the colony has not swarmed, the mother of every other
Bee in the hive is the Queen, and she is the only means
by which the population can be kept up or increased. As
on her existence and well-doing depends the vitality of
the colony, we will give her majesty precedence, and consider her natural history first.

In considering the development of the Queen, it will be
most convenient to include that of Workers and Drones,
stating the points in which they differ ; but in a great
measure the facts are applicable to all.

The egg of a Bee is of a pearly white ; it is slightly
curved, and in length several times greater than in
breadth ; it is deposited on the bottom of the cell on its
end, and stands somewhat obliquely ; there is no difference either in size or colour in Drone and Worker eggs,
*and any cluster of Worker eggs may be made to produce
Queens at the will of the Bee-master.* To the uninitiated,
this statement looks fabulous ; but I will presently
endeavour to show so clearly how it is possible, that I
think the most incredulous must be convinced. I will
even go further, and state my belief that eggs may be
taken which, uninterfered with, would produce Drones
(males), and that it is in the power of the skilful scientific
Apiarian so to act, that at his will they shall produce
either Queens, Drones, or Workers ! When we observe
a Queen in the act of ovipositing, we see her put her head
into a cell, remain a second or two, apparently inspecting
the future cradle, to see that all is in order, then, with-
drawing her head, she curves her body down into the cell,

turns half round, and, retiring, leaves an egg behind her. When she lays a considerable number, she does it equally on exactly opposite sides of the comb, thus concentrating and economizing heat for the development of the brood. Three or four days afterwards, the egg is hatched, and a small white larva or caterpillar makes its appearance; it lies coiled up and floats in a whitish transparent fluid, which is deposited in sufficient quantity by the Workers for its nourishment. The Nurse Bees now incessantly attend upon them, and they thrive and grow so rapidly that they double their size in about twelve hours, and in from four to five days they form a ring, and occupy nearly the whole length and breadth of the cell.

The Bees now seal over the cell with a cover made of wax and Bee-bread, whose colour matches that of the surrounding old combs. This cover is convex, that of the Drone cells more so than that of the Workers, and minute holes in it admit air to the larva. Like most other insects, the larva having completed its growth spins round itself a whitish silky cocoon, in which it undergoes the change to a pupa or chrysalis, and eventually in due time appears at maturity as an *imago*, or perfect insect.

 The cocoons are made of an extremely thin transparent or semi-transparent film, resembling gold-beater's skin, but without a wrinkle. This film is never removed by the bees, all other larvæ bred in the cell making new films, which remain until the capacity of the cell is sensibly reduced. These films take and retain the hexagon form of the cells most accurately. A remarkable circumstance is the perfect stretching of the film all round the wax cell; there is never found the least wrinkle or laxity, each film being intensely stretched in all parts; there is no interval whatever; the whole of each cell is lined by one entire

piece of film, without any breach, suture, or join. The
film lining the cell of the Queen Bee is considerably
thicker than the Workers', and this often is coated with
wax on the inside.

There are no such things as "Queen eggs," that is, eggs
destined from the first to produce Queens and no others;
and although the cells in which Queens are reared are
of very different construction to those of Workers and
Drones, I am of opinion that after their construction
no egg is ever laid in them; Queens are not raised by
the Workers, unless there is a probability that they will
be required either in consequence of loss, complete or
apprehended, or infertility of the old Queen; and when
the raising of Queens is decided on, the Workers select
certain eggs already laid, or even an already hatched larva
which may be as much as three days old, round which,
after destroying the contiguous cells, they build a large
cell of totally different construction, within which the
young larva is fed with a special food known to Apiarians
as Royal Jelly. This appears to have the property of
effecting a complete metamorphosis in the development
of the larva.

The food so supplied is of a stimulating character, with
an acid reaction. It is furnished to the royal larvæ in
greater quantities than can be consumed; the Bees appear
incessantly to be attending on the royal larva, so that by
this treatment the development of all its organs is much
accelerated, and on the sixteenth day from the deposition
of the egg the perfect Queen appears. When this change
is about to take place, the Bees gnaw away part of the
wax covering of the cell, until at last it becomes almost
pellucid from its extreme thinness. The marvel is in-
explicable how a mere change and greater abundance of
food, and a more roomy lodging, should so transform the

internal and external organs of any living creature.   The
case is without a parallel in all the animal creation.   It
is not a mere superficial change which has been effected,
but one which penetrates far below form and structure, to
the very fountain of life itself.   It is transformation alike
of function, of structure, and of instinct.   When a hive
becomes Queenless, instinct teaches the Bees that the loss
must be replaced, or the colony perishes.   In the natural
order of events the hive will contain eggs and young
larvæ, some of whom the Bees select for special treatment,
as above described, and rear to Queens.   That they will do
this is almost certain, but it is not so sure that the Queen
will become a prolific mother.   Between April and July
the young Queen will have every chance of meeting a
Drone on her wedding trip, but at other times the probability is more or less doubtful, and unless the desired
consummation be attained within thirty days of her birth,
she becomes a Drone breeder only—the result being the
speedy extinction of her race.   On the emergence of the
young Queen from her cell she is creamy white in colour,
her wings are limp and hairs damp, but she is in full
activity ; should she cross an open honey cell, she thrusts
in her tongue and feeds greedily, and her next thought
seems to be to destroy all others of her sister Queens who
may yet be unborn.   I have seen her tearing open their
cells before her own wings were dry, being assisted in the
murderous work by the Workers.

From two to seven days after the Queen is born, she
issues from her hive, takes wing, and after a good look
at her home and its surroundings, for after recognition,
speeds with rapid pinions on her nuptial excursion far
away out of sight.   The question naturally arises, Why
should she do this, when her own hive teems with
Drones ?   Probably it is due to the law of nature, that

forbids the mingling of kindred blood without due penalty. Did she mate at home, the usual result of breeding in and in would ensue, and in a few generations the breed would perish; but by flying far away she introduces fresh blood, and her progeny is the more vigorous. Breeders of Ligurian Queens find difficulty arise in keeping up the pure breed from the frequent mesalliances of their Queens. It is said Drones will fly four miles away from home. If Drones were not bred in large numbers, how poor would be the chance of a successful termination to her majesty's excursion. Should the Queen be unsuccessful, she will go out again and again, sometimes, alas! failing to find her way back, or perhaps get picked up by a bird; in either case, if the stock has no eggs or sufficiently young larvæ, and the state of affairs be not quickly discovered and remedied by the Bee-master, the fate of the colony is settled; it dwindles and dies. If, on the contrary, the Queen returns impregnated, she in two days usually commences her maternal duties, and never more leaves home until she accompanies a swarm and founds a new family. If a Queen Bee be dissected, in her abdominal cavity will be found, in juxtaposition, a pair of organs called the "Ovaries"; these are composed of a multitude of tubes styled the "Ovigerous Tubes," all full of eggs in every stage of growth, from

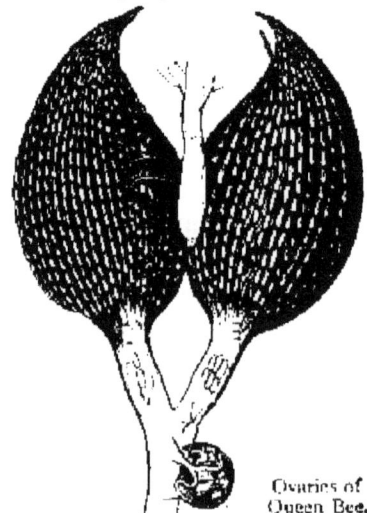

Ovaries of
Queen Bee.

the full-sized egg just ready to lay, to those that are yet very minute. All these tubes lead to a channel called the "Oviduct," each ovary having its own duct, but these soon unite into one common channel; just below this junction is a little globular sac called "the Spermatheca," about one thirty-third of an inch in diameter, covered with a beautiful white network of tracheæ, or air tubes, and communicating by a small open duct with the main oviduct, before the mouth of which every egg must pass on its passage to the cell. Like the females of most insects, the Queen Bee has sexual intercourse but once in her life, and in the act of union with the Drone the spermatheca is filled with the seminal fluid. The phenomenon that sometimes occurred in a Bee-hive of the Queen laying eggs that produced males only, had for ages puzzled philosophers without any satisfactory solution, and it was reserved for Dzierzon to promulgate a new and startling theory of reproduction, which, in the words of its distinguished author, is said to have "explained all the phenomena of the Bee-hive as perfectly as the Copernican hypothesis the phenomena of the heavens." Dzierzon first expressed his views upon the reproduction of Bees in the year 1845. The principal points of this theory may be shortly expressed thus:—1st. That the Queen (female Bee), to become good for anything (i. e. to breed Workers), must be fertilized by a Drone (the male), and that the copulation takes place only in the air; that Drone eggs do not require fecundation, but that the co-operation of the Drone is absolutely necessary when Worker Bees are to be produced; that in copulation the ovaries are not fecundated, but the seminal receptacle (or spermatheca), which in the virgin Queen is filled with a limpid fluid, is saturated with semen, after which it is more clearly distinguishable from its white colour; and that the supply of semen received during copulation is sufficient for her whole lifetime. From the inability to meet the Drone, no Queen lame in her wings can ever be perfectly fertile; that is, capable of producing both sexes. 2nd. All eggs which come to maturity in the ovaries of a Queen Bee are of one and the same kind, and when they are laid without coming in contact with the male semen become developed into male Bees. This theory of Dzierzon's, styled Parthenogenesis, has since been amply confirmed by numberless experiments, although what power the Queen possesses (or how she exercises it), of determining which eggs shall receive fecundation and which not is still a mystery. Certain it is, that when eggs are laid in Drone cells Drones are produced.

It has been suggested that the extrusion of the seminal fluid from the spermatheca requires abdominal pressure, which the construction of Worker cells affords, and the larger size of the Drone cells does not; this theory has been combated by saying the Queen will often lay eggs on the floor of cells whose walls are not yet built; but I do not know that it has been proved that these eggs were allowed by the Bees to hatch; and it is well known where eggs are dropped or placed in undesirable places they will eat them.

To demonstrate that unfertilized eggs will hatch and produce Drones, and Drones only, is easy. Observation has proved that unless a young Queen becomes impregnated during the first thirty days of her life, she becomes incapable of receiving impregnation; and though she continues laying, all her eggs produce but Drones. A Drone-breeding Queen is a common occurrence in an apiary of any extent, and is of course a misfortune, as no Workers being forthcoming to replace the dead, the

colony will become extinct.   And, again, if for the sake
of experiment the Apiarian late in the autumn causes
the Bees of a hive to rear Queens, which can be easily
done by removing their old Queen, there being no Drones
about, impregnation becomes impossible, and the young
Queen becomes a Drone breeder.   These facts are said
to be taken advantage of by breeders of Ligurian
Queens, who contrive to keep Queens in their apiaries
who breed nothing but Drones, and so they have abundance ready to fertilize late-bred Queens, when they
would otherwise naturally be unable to meet with a
mate.   It is, however, a debatable point whether Drones
from an unimpregnated Queen can fertilize another
Queen.

To dissect out the spermatheca of a Queen is an easy
task to any one who has a moderately delicate sense of
touch and a microscope.   It is only necessary with a
couple of needles to separate the last two or three seg-
ments of the abdomen, and with the needles turn out
the contents on a slip of glass.   With a magnifying
glass may now be found the little sac of a whitish-yellow
colour; and with the assistance of a microscope this
should be placed on a small drop of warm water previously put on a clean glass slip, crushed with a needle
and immediately covered with a thin glass cover, now
under a quarter of an inch objective if the Queen was
impregnated, the characteristic contorted movements of
the spermatozoa may be seen in countless thousands,
forming a strange and wonderful sight.   The spermatheca of a virgin Queen contains only a transparent
fluid.   I have verified the impregnation of a Queen Bee
months after her decease by simply soaking her abdomen
in water for a few hours, when the spermatozoa was
easily found.   My illustrious namesake, John Hunter,

the great anatomist, in conjunction with Sir Everard Home, performed a series of experiments in attempting to impregnate the eggs of Bees and other insects after they had been deposited by the female; he succeeded with the Silkworm Moth, but failed with the Bee.

The facilities we have now for such experiments are many times greater than he had; and I have thought it possible that if eggs freshly laid in Drone cells be removed to Worker cells, and then touched with a small camel-hair pencil, previously dipped in *diluted* seminal fluid obtained from the spermatheca of a Queen, the sex of the future young would be changed from male to female; and if so, Queens or Workers could be reared from them. Since I first broached this subject, I have read that Dr. Donhoff, of Germany, in 1855, reared a Worker larva from a Drone egg which he had artificially impregnated, and Langstroth tried the same experiment and failed, but he appears to have left the eggs in the Drone cells contrary to the plan of removal I suggest.

Von Siebold, who made many most skilful microscopical examinations of eggs, affirms that among fifty-two eggs taken from Worker cells, examined by him with the greatest care and conscientiousness, thirty-four furnished a positive result; namely, the existence of seminal filaments in which movements could even be detected in three eggs; and among twenty-seven eggs from Drone cells, examined with the same care and by the same method, he did not find one seminal filament in any single egg, either externally or internally.

The fertility of the Queen Bee is enormous; in this respect some greatly exceed others; a young Queen will usually lay more eggs in a given time than an old one, which is only according to the natural order of things. In the height of the summer season, with combs in good order, a Queen will lay two thousand to three thousand eggs per day, and she lives four or five years.

Dzierzon says most Queens in spacious hives, and at a favourable season, lay sixty thousand eggs in a month, and a specially fertile Queen in four years, which she on an average lives, lays over one million eggs. The rate at which eggs are deposited is largely governed by the strength of the population and the cell space at the Queen's disposal. Under the most favourable circumstances, Bees and stores abundant, hive dry, and clean empty Worker combs, in no month will breeding entirely cease. But although a hive in mild weather appears tolerably full of Bees, on the appearance of frost the Bees draw closer together, and when very cold, numbers even get quite into the vacant cells, until but a small space retains the necessary heat (from ninety to a hundred degrees Fahrenheit) to hatch eggs or rear larvæ: Of course it is useless for the Queen (were she able) to lay outside the cluster, and consequently it soon happens, from the want of warm empty cells, that breeding diminishes or ceases. At all times a daily loss of Bees by natural deaths occurs, and it is of vital importance to replace the dead by young Bees, or when spring-time arrives the hive will be found to contain only a population of old Bees, which will succumb to the first hard work.

But *one* Queen is allowed to exist in each hive, although exceptional cases have been recorded where this almost invariable rule has for a short time been broken. In four instances which have come under my personal cognizance, the dual monarchy has only been permitted to continue a few days, and in three cases out of the four it was evident the old Queen was becoming worn out and was deposed. The Queen is not nearly so bulky as a Drone, but her body is longer and considerably more tapering, more so even than that of a Worker. Her abdomen is also generally lighter in colour than the other Bees; and when she has fully entered upon her duties as a matron, her movements are slow and majestic, and she can rarely be induced to take wing. The sole business of the Queen is to lay eggs. No part of the work of the hive is done by her, and she is usually found surrounded by many of her subjects standing in a circle, with their heads towards her, ready to clean, feed, or otherwise attend to her and take care of the deposited eggs. Whenever her majesty changes her position, the Bees make way for her, closing round and keeping the circle up, allowing free space for her movements in the centre. The sight of a Queen thus attended is one of the most curious and interesting things in a hive. Old writers have been very fond of descanting on the love and veneration Bees have for their Queen, and the courage with which they will defend her. Such is not the case. I have hundreds of times picked up the Queen from the midst of crowds of her subjects, and in no instance was I ever attacked, nor could I discover any feeling of the Bees in the matter. Not unfrequently the Workers will attack their own Queen if she has been kept from the hive many minutes, and in the case of an immigration of strange Bees, they will permit the latter to seize and worry the Queen without interference. The assiduous attention paid to the Queen is evidently only Nature's care for the safety of the eggs. Until a Queen begins to lay she meets with no attention whatever from the Bees.

The Queen has a sting, but has never been known to

use it except in combat with a rival.   It has many times been related how in the case of a strange Queen's appearance in the hive, the rightful sovereign and the intruder engage in single combat, being urged thereto by the Workers.   I fear this is but a pretty fable; my experience of a great many instances being that the stranger is seized by the Workers, who gather round her and form a closely packed ball as large as a walnut, where they bite and worry her (rarely stinging) until she dies.   I have known her so kept ten days, during which time she must of course have been fed.   On the first gathering of this ball, technically called " an encasement," the Bees seem greatly excited; a continual hissing is kept up, and I have often taken the ball into my hand, and pulling off the Workers released the Queen.   The former have no inclination to sting when so treated.   If two Queens are captured and confined together under a tumbler, they run about until they meet, locked in each other's embrace, they fight and tumble about like gladiators, probably one getting soon stung, when she at once dies. At other times they meet and separate again and again, until they seem to get tired of fighting, and move indifferent to each other's presence.

The Workers form the bulk of the population, and are the smallest Bees in the hive.   Their development is complete in twenty-one days from the laying of the egg, although this period is sometimes extended or curtailed a few hours.

According to Réaumur, there are five thousand three hundred and seventy-six Workers in each pound weight, and the celebrated John Hunter counted two thousand one hundred and sixty in an imperial pint.   A populous hive will often contain forty thousand or fifty thousand Workers, whose part in the economy of the colony is, as their name implies, *to work*—by them all the labour is done: honey gathered, wax made, combs built, young tended ; in fact, everything that requires work is accomplished by the Workers. These Bees are barren, or more properly speaking, not fully developed females, which may be proved on dissection, the organs of their sex being discoverable, although not in a fully developed state. Workers have a sting, which they are ever ready to use on an enemy, even though, as is usually the case, their lives pay the penalty, for, being barbed, the sting is retained in the wound and drags out with it part of the Bee's intestines.

They are furnished with an exceedingly curious tongue, with which they obtain honey from the flowers and convey it to their mouth, whence it passes to the honey bag, to be afterwards ejected into the cells. The hind legs of the Workers are furnished with a spoon-shaped hollow, called the "Pollen Basket," in which they convey that material to the hive. The length of life of a Worker Bee is determined by the amount of work it does, and the introduction of Ligurian Queens at various seasons enables us to determine this question with almost certainty. After the introduction of a fertile Ligurian Queen to a colony of Black Workers in May, if we examine the hive two months subsequently, we shall find very few Black Bees remain, they having died and been replaced with Ligurians; and as, probably, at the time the strange Queen commenced her reign, some eggs or young larvæ of her predecessor remained, we may conclude that six weeks is the limit of time a Worker Bee will live in summer. Should the new Queen be introduced in October, not until April following will the same state of affairs be found; it is thus evident that the quietude and rest of winter prolongs the Bee's life fourfold.

"Another race the spring and fall supplies,
   They droop successive and successive rise."—EVANS.

For some time after Bees emerge from the pupa state, they employ themselves within the hive as Nurses and comb-builders; they may be readily distinguished by a greyish bloom they appear to wear.   The period of their seclusion, before they commence honey gathering, varies from a few days to two or three weeks, according to the season, they

"With fond attention guard each genial cell
   And watch the embryo, bursting from the cell."—EVANS.

It has been stated that if the Apiarian introduces a small quantity of "Royal Jelly" from a Queen cell, into a Worker cell, containing a young larva, the Bees will rear that selected larva into a Queen.

I have tried this experiment, which failed; but it is a common practice in America, when wishing to compel common bees to rear Ligurian Queens, for the Bee-master to remove the growing Black Queen larva, and replace it with a Worker larva from the Ligurian stock, which will then be successfully transformed into a Queen.

A phenomenon that sometimes happens in a Queen-less hive when a Worker is found, which is sufficiently fertile to oviposit, is surmised to occur from the Bees having partly fed it, when a larva, on Royal Jelly, causing a greater development of its sexual organs, but yet not sufficient to constitute a Queen.   These fertile Workers only produce drones, they are sometimes a great nuisance in a hive, and from the impossibility of distinguishing them from the other workers are difficult to remove.   Mr. Rorl suggests that the Bees should be driven, removed away from their stand, and allowed to fly home; the fertile Worker never having before

c

flown would not know her way home, and be probably lost.

Although I have often been conscious that a stock was suffering from the presence of a fertile Worker, only once have I had positive identification of the individual. A correspondent having captured a Worker in the act of ovipositing, forwarded her to me alive—outwardly I could see no difference from an ordinary Worker, but on dissection found eggs in various stages of development.

The Drones are the males, whose sole office is to fertilize the young Queens; although doubtless they assist in keeping up the temperature of the hive. They are much stouter than either the Queen or the Workers, but do not exceed the Queen in length. They have no sting with which to defend themselves, no basket on their legs for pollen, no excretory organs for wax, and no suitable tongue for gathering honey from the flowers. Their voice is a loud sonorous hum, very noticeable when flying. Under ordinary circumstances, they only exist in the summer, when young Queens may be expected to emerge; and a colony having sent forth its complement of swarms, the Drones are immediately slaughtered by the Workers; they accomplish this butchery by biting, teasing, and starving their unfortunate brothers, for they seem to know that if they use their stings they themselves will die. Often a Drone may be seen with two or more Workers gnawing at his wings and legs; then, thrown from the hive, he perishes for want of power to rise again. While the massacre is in full progress, the floor of the hive may be found covered with wounded Drones in various stages of starvation, kept there by the Bees until they die or can be thrown out.

" The sad-ey'd justice with his surly hum,
Delivering o'er to executors pale,
The lazy, yawning Drone."—SHAKESPEARE.

When suffering this ill treatment Drones will take refuge in any neighbouring hives, and where one is Queenless they will be welcomed and allowed to remain unmolested. The number of Drones in a hive varies considerably from one hundred or two hundred to some thousands.

I do not know that the length of life of the Drone has been satisfactorily ascertained—in fact, we may conclude they usually meet with a violent death before they are three months old, but I have in a Queenless stock kept Drones alive from Autumn until the following Spring. Drones, the progeny of a fertile Worker, are commonly reared in Worker cells; in this case they are diminutive in size—scarcely larger than Workers. The act of copulation with the Queen is instantly fatal to the Drone, and in separating, the Queen drags out his organs, which remain attached to her for some time after her return home.

The possession of a hive of Bees affords a fund of material by which many instructive and amusing experiments may be carried out, and by which facts in natural history may be brought to light, perhaps small in themselves, but great in the aggregate.

Sir John Lubbock has initiated such experiments in endeavouring to arrive at a knowledge of how far Bees are endowed with power of communicating intelligence one to another—his conclusions are not very favourable to the Bees; I give the Bees more credit for that power than he does, but have made no special observations to demonstrate the point. In a paper communicated to the Linnean Society, Sir John Lubbock states, he arrives at the conclusion, that Bees do not communicate intelligence of discovered food one to the other, and that they do not readily discover honey. Probably Sir John's experiments were conducted in summer, when Bees are perfectly indifferent to exposed stores. I think the same experiments carried on in Autumn, after all natural supplies had ceased, would have shown the experimentalist the desperate eagerness of the Bees for plunder; that they have means of communicating intelligence of a discovery I have little doubt. In my Apiary I have seen a bottle of syrup, placed on the top of a hive containing Ligurian Bees, surrounded and emptied in a few hours, by an only stock of Black Bees standing in the midst of ten hives of Ligurians, scarcely one of the latter ever being seen in the crowd; how else than the power of communication can we account for the Black Bees from the solitary hive taking possession, unless they had been led thither by the first discoverers, their compatriots?

That Bees can see of course does not admit of doubt. When a Bee leaves her hive for the first time, she flies backwards and forwards several times with her head turned towards it—evidently taking its bearings for recognition; and then, however far she flies, returns straight home; now if before her return the appearance of the hive be altered, she becomes evidently confused, but eventually enters; if the hive be moved but a few inches, she gives the same indication of doubt, and will, if possible, alight on the old spot several times before she discovers her home; the acuteness of her sight does not, as we should think would be the case, direct her at once to the hive she has been accustomed to, but I should rather say it is instinct that guides her to the old spot. Sir John Lubbock, who has experimented very patiently on the senses of Bees, took considerable trouble to ascertain if Bees can distinguish colour, and he comes to an affirmative conclusion.

Naturalists have many times observed that insects, ants especially, communicate intelligence one to the other by crossing their antennæ ; and Huber states that in Bees these organs have the same use.   He wished to ascertain whether, when the Bees had lost a Queen (intelligence of which traverses a whole hive in about an hour), they discovered the sad event by their smell, their touch, or any unknown means.   He first divided a hive by a grate which kept the two portions about a quarter of an inch apart, so that the Bees could not come at each other.   Though scent would pass in that part in which there was no Queen, the Bees were soon in great agitation, and as they did not discover her where she was confined, in a short time they began Queen cells, which quieted them.   He next separated them by a partition through which they could pass their antennæ but not their heads ; in this case the Bees all remained tranquil, neither intermitting the care of the brood, nor abandoning their other employments, nor did they begin any royal cell.   The way they assured themselves that their Queen was in the vicinity, and to communicate with her was, to pass their antennæ through the openings of the grate.   An infinite number of these organs might be seen at once, as it were, searching in all directions, and the Queen was observed answering these anxious inquiries of her subjects in the most marked manner, for she was always fastened by her feet to the grate, crossing her antennæ with those of the inquirers.

Notwithstanding the conclusion of Huber, it is not uncommon for bees to build Queen cells, even when a Queen is with them confined in a wire gauze cage, where they could have free communication with her by means of their antennæ.

That the antennæ of insects are organs of intelligence is generally admitted, but in what manner intelligence is communicated has never been determined, probably through a sense of which we know nothing, and never shall, any more than light can be comprehended by those born blind. The olfactory sense is highly developed in Bees; by it they discover food, and know one another. But the sense of hearing is, probably, not very acute. The piping of an imprisoned Queen appears to be heard by the reigning monarch, as she seems to answer it; but Sir John Lubbock, in relating his experiments, tells us that with the utmost efforts he could make with tuning-forks, whistles, violin, or shouting close to the head of the Bee, when all around was still, he never could obtain the slightest indication that the sounds were heard.

Messrs. Kirby and Spence, in their admirable work, thus describes a Bee's operations on a flower when gathering nectar:—

" Observe a Bee that has alighted upon an open flower. The hum produced by the motion of her wing ceases, and her employment begins. In an instant she unfolds her tongue, which was before rolled up under her head; with what rapidity does she dart this organ between the petals and the stamens! At one time she extends it to its full length, then she contracts it; she moves it about in all directions, so that it may be applied both to the concave and convex surface of a petal, and wipe them both, and thus, by a virtuous theft, robs it of all its nectar. All the while this is going on, she keeps herself n a constant vibratory motion. The object of the industrious insect is not like the more selfish butterfly, to appropriate this treasure to herself. It goes into the honey bag as into a laboratory, where it is transformed into pure honey; and when she returns to the hive she regurgitates it in this form into one of the cells appropriated to that purpose, in order that after tribute is paid from it to the Queen, it may constitute a supply of food for the rest of the community."

Virgil asserted, "a Bee is a ray of divinity;" and when studying with awe the wonders of the Bee-hive, so beautiful in their simplicity, so perfect in their ends, can we fail to acknowledge the presence of that All-guiding Hand, who, by these little insects and all their wondrous works, teaches man a lesson of industry, forethought, and order.

COMBS.

"Galleries of Art, and Schools of Industry."

COMBS, as everyone knows, are built by the Bees of wax, which is a natural secretion of the builders and appears in fine scales between their abdominal rings; it is eliminated from honey, or other saccharine food, possibly assisted by a simultaneous consumption of Bee bread. It was formerly believed that Bees secreted wax from pollen, which we now know to be wrong, from the much greater facilities for observation we enjoy.

After a hard day's work in honey gathering the Bees do not rest, but employ the night in comb-building; this work being then chiefly carried on, and on days when the weather forbids out-door employment; thus no time is lost, even if they be confined several days. If the combs of a hive are examined, the cells will be found to be hexagonal—of several sizes—those for Drones and

Workers never vary, the first are about seventeen to the linear inch, the latter twenty-seven. As well as being used for breeding, these cells are brought into requisition for honey storing indiscriminately if occasion arises; there are also honey cells proper, generally of elongated Drone construction, sometimes very deep, in supers even two or three inches—these honey cells in the main hive are usually found at the top and sides of combs, and on the outer combs more than on the central ones which form the brood nest. Queen cells, which are only present occasionally, that is, when Queens are necessary to be reared, if formed of the Bees' own accord, will be mostly found on the margin of the combs; if the Queen-rearing is forced, they are more often in the centre. These cells are, when fully formed, of an elongated egg shape, one inch long by half an inch in diameter; and, contrary to the other cells, which have a slight upward tendency, these always open at the bottom, that is, mouth downwards. The number of Queens that the stock has reared may commonly be known by the bases of the old Queen cells left; they appear much after the shape of the acorn cup. Cells, where the young Queen has been destroyed by the reigning monarch, are usually quite cleared away by the Workers. Queen cells are never used twice.

The process of comb-building is thus described by Huber (I may here say that in his time it was thought there were two kinds of Workers, whom he styles Wax Makers and Nurses; the fact is, there is but one kind; but the newly-born Workers, for some time after birth, confine their work to nursing and comb-building, and do not at first issue from the hive to gather honey) :—

"The Wax Makers, having taken a due portion of honey or sugar, from either of which wax can be elaborated, suspend themselves to each other, the claws of the fore-legs of the lowermost being attached to those of the hind pair of the uppermost, and form themselves into a cluster, the exterior layer of which looks like a kind of curtain. This cluster consists of a series of festoons or garlands which cross each other in all directions, and in which most of the Bees turn their back upon the observer ; the curtain has no other motion than what it receives from the interior layers, the fluctuations of which are communicated to it. All this time the Nurse Bees preserve their wonted activity and pursue their usual employments. The Wax Makers remain immovable for about twenty-four hours, during which period the formation of wax takes place ; and thin laminæ of this material may be generally perceived under their abdomen. One of these Bees is now seen to detach itself from one of the central garlands of the cluster, to make a way amongst its companions to the middle of the vault or top of the hive, and by turning itself round to form a kind of void, in which it can move itself freely. It then suspends itself to the centre of the space which it has cleared, the diameter of which is about an inch ; it next seizes one of the laminæ of wax with a pincer formed by the posterior metatarsus and tibia, and drawing it from beneath the abdominal segment, one of the anterior legs takes it with its claws and carries it to the mouth. This leg holds the lamina with its claws vertically, the tongue rolled up serving for a support, and by elevating or depressing it at will, causes the whole of its circumference to be exposed to the action of the mandibles, so that the margin is soon gnawed into pieces, which drop as they are detached into the double cavity, bordered with hairs, of the mandibles. These fragments, pressed by others newly separated, fall on one side of the mouth and issue from it in the form of a very narrow riband.

"They are then presented to the tongue, which impregnates them with a frothy liquor like a bouilli. During this operation the tongue assumes all sorts of forms: sometimes it is flattened like a spatula, then like a trowel, which applies itself to the riband of wax; at other times it resembles a pencil terminating in a point. After having moistened the whole of the riband, the tongue pushes it so as to make it re-enter the mandibles, but in an opposite direction, where it is worked up anew. The liquor mixed with the wax communicates to it a whiteness and opacity which it had not before; and the object of this mixture of bouilli, which did not escape the observation of Réaumur, is, doubtless, to give it that ductility and tenacity which it possesses in its perfect state.

"The Foundress Bee, the name which this first beginner of a comb deserves, next applies these prepared parcels of wax against the vault of the hive, disposing them with the point of her mandibles in the direction which she wishes them to take; and she continues these manœuvres until she has employed the whole lamina that she had separated from her body, when she takes a second proceeding in the same manner. She gives herself no care to compress the molecules of wax which she has heaped together; she is satisfied if they adhere to each other. At length she leaves her work and is lost in the crowd of her companions. Another succeeds and resumes the employment; then a third; all follow the same plan of placing their little masses; and if any, by chance, gives them a contrary direction, another coming removes them to their proper place. The result of all these operations is a mass or little wall of wax, with uneven surfaces, five or six lines long, two lines high, and half a line thick, which descends perpendicularly below the vault of the hive. In this first work is no angle nor any trace of the figure of the cells. It is a simple partition in a right line without any inflection.

"The Wax Makers having thus laid a foundation of a comb, are succeeded by the Nurse Bees, which are alone competent to model and perfect the work.

"The former are the labourers, who convey the stone and mortar; the latter, the masons, who work them up into the form which the intended structure requires. One of the Nurse Bees now places itself horizontally on the vault of the hive, its head corresponding to the centre of the mass or wall which the Wax Makers have left, and which is to form the partition of the comb into two opposite assemblages of cells; and, with its mandibles rapidly moving its head, it moulds in that side of the wall a cavity which is to form the base of one of the cells to the diameter of which it is equal. When it has worked some minutes it departs, and another takes its place, deepening the cavity, heightening its lateral margins by heaping up the wax to right and left by means of its teeth and fore feet, and giving them a more upright form; more than twenty Bees successively employ themselves in this work. When arrived at a certain point, other Bees begin on the yet untouched and opposite side of the mass, and, commencing the bottom of two cells, are in turn relieved by others. While still engaged in this labour, the Wax Makers return, and add to the mass, augmenting its extent in every way, the Nurse Bees again continuing their operations. After having worked the bottom of the cells of the first row into their proper forms, they polish them, and give them their finish, while others begin the outline of a new series.

"The cells themselves, or prisms, which result from the reunion and meeting of the sides, are next constructed. These are engrafted on the borders of the cavities hollowed in the mass; the Bees begin them by making the contour of the bottoms, which at first is unequal, of equal height; thus all the margins of the cells offer an uniformly level surface from their first origin, and until they have acquired their proper length. The sides are heightened in an order analogous to that which the insects follow in finishing the bottoms of the cells; and the length of these tubes is so perfectly proportioned that there is no observable inequality between them. It is to be remarked that though the general form of the cells is hexagonal, that of those first begun is pentagonal, the side next the top of the hive, and by which the comb is attached, being much broader than the rest, whence the comb is more strongly united to the hive, than if these cells were of the ordinary shape. It, of course, follows that the base of these cells, instead of being formed like those of the hexagonal cells, of three rhomboids, consist of one rhomboid and two trapeziums.

"The form of a new comb is lenticular, its thickness always diminishing towards the edges. This gradation is constantly observable, whilst it keeps enlarging in circumference; but as soon as the Bees get sufficient space to lengthen it, it begins to lose this form and to assume parallel surfaces; it has then received the shape which it will always preserve.

"The Bees appear to give the proper forms to the bottoms of the cells, by means of their antennæ, which extraordinary organs they seem to employ as directors, by which their other instruments are instructed to execute a very complete work. They do not remove a single particle of wax until the antennæ have explored the surface that is to be sculptured. By the use of these organs, which are so flexible and so readily applied to all parts, however delicate, that they can perform the functions of compasses in measuring very minute objects, they can work in the dark, and raise those wonderful combs, the first production of insects.

" Every part of the work appears a natural consequence of that which precedes it, so that chance has no share in the admirable results witnessed. The Bees cannot depart from their prescribed route, except in consequence of particular circumstances, which alter the basis of their labour. The original mass of wax is never augmented, but by an uniform quantity; and what is most astonishing, this augmentation is made by the Wax Makers, who are the depositories of the primary matter, and possess not the art of sculpturing the cells.

" The Bees never begin two masses for combs at the same time; but scarcely are some rows of cells constructed in the first, when two other masses, one on each side of it, are established at equal distances from it, and parallel to it, and then again two more exterior to these. The combs are always enlarged and lengthened in a progression, proportioned to the priority of their origin, the middle comb being constantly advanced beyond the two adjoining ones by some rows of cells, and they beyond those that are exterior to them. Was it permitted to these insects to lay the foundation of all their combs at the same time, they could not be placed conveniently or parallel to the other. So with respect to the cells, the first cavity determines the place of all that succeed it.

" A large number of Bees work at the same time on the same comb; but they are not moved to it by a simultaneous, but by a successive impulse. A single Bee begins every partial operation, and many others in succession add their efforts to hers, each appearing to act individually in a direction impressed either by the Workers who have preceded it, or by the condition in which it finds the work.   The whole population of Wax Makers is in a state of the most complete inaction, till one Bee goes forth to lay the foundations of the first comb.   Immediately others second her intentions, adding to the height and length of the mass; and when they cease to act, a Bee, if the term may be used, of another profession, one of the Nurse Bees, goes to form the draft of the first cell, in which she is succeeded by others."

In the form of construction of the cells an abstruse mathematical problem is involved, which long taxed the powers of our ablest mathematicians to solve, and yet· this problem the Bee, inspired by a Teacher who never errs, solves every time a comb is built.   The combs of a Bee-hive are formed in parallel vertical strata, each of which, when of worker construction, is about an inch in thickness (drone comb is somewhat thicker), the distance between the surfaces of adjoining strata being about half an inch, a space which allows for the passage of the bees over both surfaces.   The combs generally extend the whole breadth of the hive, from front to rear, and nearly the whole length from top to bottom; they consist of thin partitions which enclose hexagonal cells opening on both surfaces of the comb, and closed by a partition which is common to those on both sides, and occupies the middle distance between the two surfaces.   This partition is not, however, a plane, but is composed of a collection, of rhombs ; three and sometimes four of these rhombs incline to one another at a certain angle from the bottom of each cell, which thus has the shape of a flattened pyramid, of which the base is toward the mouth of the cell; the axis of each cell coincides not with the axis of the cell on the opposite surface, but with one of its angles, so that each of the three obtuse angles, at the base of the terminal pyramid, corresponds to the central parts of three of the cells on the opposite side. We may easily satisfy ourselves that such is the case, by piercing the centres of each of the three planes which close the bottom of a cell with a pin, when on turning the comb the three pins will be found to have passed into three different cells on the opposite side. No one has yet been able to explain how bees could have adopted and adhered to so regular a plan of architecture, and what principles can actuate so great a multitude to co-operate by the most effectual and systematic mode in its completion. Several theories have been promulgated, but none have borne the test of serious examination. The foundations of the combs are laid by the bees raising a solid block or plate of wax of a semi-circular form. In this they scoop out a small vertical channel of the size of an ordinary cell. The sides of this channel are then strengthened by additions of wax. On the opposite side two other channels are formed, one on each side of the plane opposite to the former channel. The extremities of these channels, which first present a curved outline, are then fashioned into straight walls forming an angle at each vertex. The bottom of each cell being thus sketched out, the design is completed by raising walls round the sides. Different bees generally work on the opposite sides at the same time, and appear to have some perception of the thickness of the partitions and of the situation of the opposite walls, in which they are perhaps guided by strong prominences occasioned by the depressions which correspond to them on the other side ; and they scrape off the wax in those places where its thickness is greatest, that is, where the bees on the other side had accumulated materials. Soon after the bees have completed the foundations, and constructed a few of the cells of the central comb, they begin two others, one on each side at the proper distance, and in this manner continue to form others in succession, in proportion as the former are advanced. Their object at first seems to be to extend the surface of the work, so as to admit of the greatest possible number of workers being employed at one and the same time. In this way, then, the work proceeds from all points at once; new cells being begun before the former are completed, so that the comb, while it is in progress of construction, has a semi-lenticular shape, broader at the top and tapering below and towards the sides. It extends downwards, however, more rapidly than in any other direction, and its surfaces do not become parallel to each other till the last stage of the building process. When this is completed, the whole is further strengthened by an addition of propolis round the margin of all the cells, and the junctions of every plane, both of the sides and bottoms of the cells, are soldered together by a lining of the same substance. The cells when new are white, but become gradually darker, and when very ancient are almost black; and when in this condition the capacity of the cells is so reduced, by the accumulation of cast-off cocoons, as sensibly to diminish the size of the bees bred therein, but the combs are quite good for breeding purposes for five or six years.

> "So work the Honey Bees,
> Creatures that by a rule in Nature, teach
> The art of order to a peopled kingdom."—SHAKESPEARE.

BEE-KEEPING.

"As each for the good of the whole is bent,
  And stores up his treasures for all,
We hope for an evening, with hearts content,
For the winter of life without lament.
That summer is gone with its hours misspent,
  And the harvest is past recall!"—DR. AIKIN.

A TRAVELLER who has much acquaintance with Continental rural life, cannot fail to be impressed, when journeying in England, with the small number of Beehives he sees scattered about, amongst either the cottages of the labouring classes, or the farms and courts of the gentry, compared with what he sees abroad; and when, perchance, his eye alights on a hive or two, he will nine times out of ten find only the ancient straw skep in use, and that probably badly made. The cottager, although now used to the innovation of steam ploughs and thrashing machines, has been quite content to jog on with his Bees in the same manner that his Saxon forefathers did a thousand years ago. But what a life, and *what a death* for the poor Bees!—the hives are probably reeking with moisture, dirty and decayed, and when the industrious labourers have, in spite of all such disadvantages and neglect, filled them with Nature's luscious gifts, the fate in store for them is suffocation, with the horrible fumes of brimstone; and this procedure is not practised by the poor and ignorant only, but in many cases adopted by the educated and opulent if, by chance, they own a few Bees.

"Ah! see where, robbed and murdered in that pit,
  Lies the still-heaving hive, at evening snatched,
Beneath the cloud of guilt-concealing night,
And fixed o'er sulphur while not dreaming ill,

D

The happy people in their waxen cells
Sat tending public cares.
Sudden, the dark, oppressive steam ascends,
And used to milder scents, the tender race
By thousands tumble from their honied dome
Into a gulf of blue sulphurous flame."—THOMSON.

Tell an ignorant labourer that his honey can be got from the hive, his Bees preserved to work for him again, and that no more honey will be required to feed twenty thousand than ten thousand little mouths during the winter, and you would simply elicit an incredulous smile, he certainly would not be induced to try, however lucidly the process was explained; but *show him how to do it,* let him see the result, and he will another year, perhaps, follow the example set, greatly to his own benefit as well as to that of his Bees. To all Bee-keepers who are thinking men or women, I commend the following chapters, which, carefully studied, will give every necessary instruction by which they may become accomplished Apiarians, and a centre of knowledge for the enlightenment of others.

What portion of our fertile land does not afford sustenance for Bees? Mr. Alfred Neighbour in his work, *The Apiary,* devotes a chapter to "Bee-keeping in London." Could we ever imagine a more unpromising field for honey gathering—London!—foggy, smoky London! But think a moment; London has parks, squares, gardens; and each of these has trees, flowers, and shrubs. What matters if the flowers be dirty, their nectaries secrete the coveted sweet, and the natural filter of the Bees will clarify it better than any artificial one could do. A lady living in Kensington, told me she kept Bees there; they throve well, and had furnished her with a super of fourteen pounds weight!—they are also kept in the busy Strand next to Charing Cross Railway Station.

It has been asserted that Bees will fly five or six miles for honey, if a supply nearer home be not obtainable; they may, but such an extreme labour would not allow the stock to thrive. Too much time and muscular strength would be consumed in making the journey. The great danger to Bees in town is their liability to be tempted into shops, such as grocers, confectioners, &c., where they get bewildered, fly to the window, and, in the vain attempt to penetrate the glass, they die. Breweries are also fatal places, the sweet wort attracting numbers who perish by drowning.

Associations and societies for the encouragement of agriculture, horticulture, and various other sister sciences, have for many years abounded in England, but it was reserved for 1874, to see the establishment of the first one for the encouragement and promotion of Bee-keeping, when the British Bee-keepers' Association, presided over by Sir John Lubbock, sprung into existence, through the exertions of nearly all our own leading Apiarians, whose observations and writings have contributed so largely to apiarian science. The Association, which did me the honour to elect me Honorary Secretary, held an exhibition at the Crystal Palace, in September, 1874, of " Hives, Bees, and their Produce," of far greater magnitude than was ever gathered together in Great Britain before ; these Exhibitions have been continued at the same place, the Alexandra Palace, and at South Kensington, besides giving birth to many Provincial Associations and Exhibitions, the result being that Bee-Keeping in England has received an impetus, which, it is hoped, will eventually be productive of great good.

Such competitive exhibitions surpass everything else as a means of improving all sciences, and the present advanced state of agriculture and horticulture, is mainly attributable to them. Apiarian Exhibitions form no exception, an immense interest is excited in Bee-keeping, and multitudes of persons have vowed to keep Bees, pleased and astonished at sight of the wonderful supers of honey, and the interesting practical demonstrations of Bee management that are shown, where the Bees, thanks to the skill, coolness, and courage of the manipulators, seem to set aside all will of their own, obedient only to that of their masters. The aim of the Association is, to make these Exhibitions Annual, and to further, by a variety of other means, the advancement of Bee-keeping, both as a Natural Science, and as a means of bettering the condition of cottagers, and the agricultural labouring classes, as well as the advocacy of humanity to the industrious labourer, the Honey Bee. The expenses naturally attendant on these efforts to do good, although not heavy (no officers being paid), can only be met by the addition of members to the ranks of the Association, and the hearty co-operation of all Bee-keepers. Let no one, therefore, stand aloof, but contribute his mite both of money and goodwill to aid the progression of Bee-keeping.

Many persons reading my account of how the Bees may be used will naturally feel surprised, and, perhaps, doubt that their own courage or skill could ever arrive at a point that would enable them to remove all the Bees from a hive, shovel them up or drive them about wherever they desire them to go, and will, perhaps, think they might as well be told to enter a lions' den and put the noble beasts through their performances after seeing the keeper do so. To those unaccustomed to Bees the doubt is reasonable ; but there is no secret or charlatanism in the matter. A certain amount of courage must be present with coolness and quietness; the rest is easy if my instructions are followed. During many practical expositions of Apiarian manipulations more than one lady has been courageously present in the manipulating room, by their own choice, without receiving any injury, although thousands of Bees, driven from their hives, were crawling and flying all round, while the spectators behind a glass or gauze screen gazed with astonishment both at the Bees and the ladies. The facility of handling Bees is not of modern origin. A century ago, a Bee-keeper, named Daniel Wildman, who was domiciled in Holborn, astonished London by his performances with these insects. He had an exhibition at Islington, the records of which, although we must take them "with a grain of salt," show that he had a considerable acquaintance with the fears and dispositions of Bees. It is said he could cause a swarm to settle almost instantaneously where he pleased, even on his head, remove them to his hand, a window, table, &c., at pleasure. This seemed wonderful; but the solution was simply possession of the Queen—where she went, there went the Bees! To keep Bees in a merciful and rational manner it is by no means necessary to undertake all the operations I describe, or even adopt frame hives. If the rudest form of hive, the straw skep, be maintained, it is yet not at all necessary to destroy the Bees to get their honey. Read and master the one chapter on "Driving," and the Bee-keeper can rifle their stores, yet preserve their lives and strengthen his stocks for next year, so that they will be able to do double work in reward for their master's humanity.

> "Leave them happy in their copious store,
> A part they'll give; and why desire ye more?
> And must ye kill? Mistaken thought—ah!—shame,
> No more involve them in sulphurous flame."

Cottagers can, if they desire it, gradually master all manipulations in time. Gentlemen who are already adepts will willingly give all the help in their power. The cottagers of Scotland far exceed the English in the ability they display in Bee-keeping. The country gentleman desirous of helping his poorer neighbours, cannot do a better thing than furnish pattern improved hives supplemented, if need be, by a swarm of Bees, and show how they are to be managed. The Bees may be repaid out of their increase.

When an Apiarian can handle his Bees with impunity, their study becomes a fascinating pursuit, their doings are so truly wonderful—the temptation to inhale the fresh air and watch the Bees becomes too strong to be resisted, a man's mind and knowledge expand from the wonders he beholds. New friends are made, ideas are interchanged, inventive faculties are set in motion to fashion some aid for the Bees or their master, and many are the delights that spring from the contemplation of the busy throng. And then the children !—what delight they exhibit to see the busy Workers set out or return from their labours in the fields ; what lessons in mercy do they receive when they pick up the poor little Bees who, returning to their hives, fall chilled to the ground. Children are easily taught not to hurt the Bees, and they then discover the Bees will not hurt them. My own little ones, when two or three years old, would stand before the hives peering into the entrance quite unmolested, and at my bidding allow the Bees to crawl over their hands—knowing they would receive no injury. Fear for the children need never deter any one from keeping Bees.

Amongst all naturalists there is a kind of Free-masonry which makes welcome the visit of any person with similar tastes; and should the Bee-keeper, who is desirous of learning more, find himself in the neighbourhood of a scientific Apiarian, let me counsel him to pay the latter a visit; he will, I am sure, be truly welcome to a sight of the Apiary and a friendly chat, which must be barren indeed if both parties do not part wiser men. Many years ago, as an entomologist, I collected insects of another order. Whenever I found myself in a strange locality my first inquiry was for others of a similar taste on whom I made a point of calling—need I say I never met with a rebuff, but, on the contrary, made many pleasant friends.

One of the principal writers on the Bee was Francis Huber, an eminent naturalist of the last and present century. *He was totally blind;* yet even this great deprivation did not hinder him from becoming the greatest and most accurate observer of Bees that had ever then lived. His observations were made with the eyes and assistance of his servant, Francis Burnens, who, although a peasant, was a man of great talent, possessing indefatigable energy and enthusiasm; Huber was also assisted by his wife. His observations and deductions made, although many of them have since been proved incorrect, gave to the world a wonderful store of facts hitherto unsuspected, and laid the foundation for the labours of many naturalists of later times. His "leaf hive" was the first frame hive; it was very valuable for observation purposes, and is yet often used, although not so convenient as some newer inventions.

Wise little creatures are Bees!—for they seem to be warned of the approach of bad weather by some particular instinct; it sometimes happens when multitudes are abroad very busy, they will on a sudden cease from their work; not a single one stirs out, and those that are away hurry home in such crowds that the entrance of the hive is too small to admit them.   On such an occasion, look to the sky, and you will, probably, discover some of those black clouds that denote impending rain.   Whether the Bees see the clouds gathering, as some imagine, or whether they feel some other effects of the change on their bodies, is not yet determined ; but it is asserted that no Bee is ever caught in a sudden shower, unless it be at a very great distance from the hive, or injured by accident.   Searching for wild Honey Bees in England would, I am afraid, be an unprofitable task.   In many country districts Bees are known to be located in certain hollow trees or roofs of houses ; but the proprietors, although, perhaps, they would be glad to get rid of the Bees, would not so readily allow their house to be dismantled or their tree to be cut down.   In America, however, they are not so particular, and many men make a living " Bee-hunting ; " others who do not follow it as a calling do not fail to take advantage of the lucky find when it occurs.

The time that Bees will inhabit some stations is wonderful.   Thorley tells us that a swarm took possession of a spot under the leads of Ludovicus Vives, in Oxford, where they continued one hundred and ten years, from 1520 to 1630.

Bee-keeping is more or less carried on in all civilized and many semi-civilized countries ; from the cold inhospitable region of Siberia, to the sultry shores of Africa, we may find Bee-hives often in vast numbers.   Spain teems with them ; in the rural districts they are everywhere found, as also in Russia where, in the province of Yekarterinoslaw, there are nearly four hives to every human being.

In former times, Poland was celebrated for its Bee-culture, and is still so now to some extent in the province of Lublin, it having everywhere else fallen into decay. The reason why Bee-keeping is so industriously carried on in Russia is twofold. Firstly, because the peasants use honey instead of sugar; and secondly, because wax tapers to the value of 1,200,000 rubles (nearly £182,500) are required for the churches. Buschen states the quantity of honey annually produced in European Russia to be 600,000 to 700,000 pud (9,643 to 11,250 tons), and a proportionate quantity of wax.

In the United States, apiculture is carried on largely, both as a distinct trade and adjunct to other farming, with a great amount of scientific attention. Many of our most valuable apicultural improvements and inventions have had their origin there, and in no other country would the old straw skep and death-and-brimstone system meet with greater contempt.

Within this last 25 years, California has become a great country for Bee-culture. In 1876, Mr. Harbison reached New York with his honey crop, from his six Apiaries in San Diego. The shipment consisted of ten car-loads, or 200,000 lbs. of honey. In Les Angelos county, we are told, there are 200 Apiaries with over 12,000 hives, from which over 500,000 lbs. of honey are taken annually. The income of Mr. J. S. Harbison, derived from honey alone, is said to be more than £5000 per annum, clear of all expenses. In the State of New York, Captain Hetherington of Cherry Valley, sold in 1874 over 58,000 lbs. of honey, from his own Apiaries, and Adam Grimm of Jefferson as much more. Many more examples of large products in the United States could be cited.

Germany, too, boasts of many Bee-keepers; in comparison with that Empire, Great Britain is far behind. Here, where one hive is kept, we might have a thousand;

where one pound of honey is gathered, a ton is wasted. Vast quantities of honey are annually imported from France and the West Indies which should be supplied by our own rural labouring population who, in addition, might, as I have above stated they do in Russia, use it in lieu of sugar. According to the best authorities, it is impossible to overstock a neighbourhood with Bees—at least it never has been done—and, therefore, we may conclude there is no danger here. In Germany, many Apiaries contain in close proximity 200 to 300 hives. Ehrenfels had 1000 in three separate establishments, but sufficiently near together that he could visit them all in half an hour's ride. In Russia and Hungary, Apiaries numbering from 2000 to 3000 hives are not infrequent, and as many as 4000 are often congregated together at one point on the heaths of Germany. It is calculated that in Hanover there are 141 hives to each square mile, and a German writer alleges, that the Bees of Lunenberg pay all the taxes assessed on their proprietors, and leave a surplus besides—this in a district so barren that it has been called the Arabia Petrea of Germany.

In former times, the Island of Corsica, comprising 3790 square miles, paid to Rome an annual tribute of 200,000 pounds of wax, which presupposes a production of two to three million pounds of honey; and East Friesland, a province of Holland, maintains at the present day an average of 2000 hives per square mile. These statistics could be indefinitely increased, and they show that, comparatively, Great Britain is bare of Bees. I question if we have *one* colony to a square mile.

Oettl says: "When a large flock of sheep is grazing on a limited area, there may soon be a deficiency of pasturage. But this cannot be the case with Bees, as a good honey district cannot be readily overstocked by them. To-day, when the air is moist and warm, the plants may yield a superabundance of nectar; while to-morrow, being cold and wet, there may be a total want of it. When there is sufficient heat and moisture, the saccharine juices of plants will readily fill the nectaries, and be as quickly replenished when carried off by the Bees. Every cold night checks the flow of honey, and every clear warm day reopens the fountain. "*The flowers expanded to-day, must be visited while open, for if left to wither, their stores are lost.* Bees cannot collect to-morrow what is left ungathered to-day."

How long shall it continue to be said that we thus allow God's gifts to be wasted before our eyes? This has become an age of utilization. See the multitude of formerly "waste" products that are now made useful; and yet, throughout the length and breadth of this flowery land:

"Full many a flower is born to blush unseen,
And waste its fragrance on the desert air."—GRAY.

I appeal, therefore, to the clergymen, the country gentlemen, and all those who, by their rank and position, are looked up to, and have influence with the labouring classes, and would say to them: Encourage by every means in your power the spread and growth of Bee-keeping. Teach by the force of example what satisfactory results may be obtained by improved hives, and a more sensible and humane policy towards our interesting and industrious little fellow-labourers; let it be seen that the produce of a dozen hives, with little labour, and scarcely any outlay, will suffice to pay the rent or find shoes for the little ones; and in the course of a few years, we shall find no cottage without its hive or hives, and the old barbarous system of Bee slaughter will be quite a thing of the past.

When a man thinks of starting Bee-keeping, he generally has an eye to profit, and the question is commonly asked : " How much honey shall I get per hive ? " Now this question is more easily asked than answered, the result being dependent on so many circumstances over some of which we have no control. Moreover, many think they have only to obtain a hive of Bees, set it down in the garden, and giving it no further attention, profit must, as a matter of course, ensue. This is a great mistake ; the farmer sows his seed with the same end in view, "profit." Nature makes the seeds to grow, but without attention from the farmer but a poor crop would be gathered in. We buy poultry, feed and attend them, and profit by their eggs and increase, but we get none of these advantages without a proper share of attention and expenditure. Thus with Bee-keeping ; thousands of Bee-keepers in England, belonging to the agricultural labouring classes, keep Bees, give them the minimum of attention, and make but small profit ; and the educated Bee-keeper, unless he follow a more rational plan, must not expect a better result.

Mr. Pettigrew, in his ' Handy Book on Bees,' wherein he advocates the use of straw skeps only, talks of the contents of these hives commonly weighing from 100 to 150 pounds, and instances a swarm in its first season reaching 160 pounds in weight; he also states that at a village in Lanarkshire, the profits of Bee-keeping averaged in six consecutive years, £2 11s. 8d. per hive. I can only say I never saw such hives, and none have made their appearance at the British Beekeepers' Association's Shows, where they could not have failed to take many prizes; and the Beekeeper who allows his expectations to rise to this height, will be grievously disappointed, more especially if he repudiate the use of all the improvements of modern times, the result of the collective experience and wisdom of able and truth-telling observers. Very strong stocks have been known to gather 10 or 12 pounds per day during exceptionally good honey weather; and a skilful Apiarian in a good honey locality and season, by the expenditure of ceaseless care and attention, may, perchance, with a strong stock of Bees, obtain a super of 80 or 100 pounds of pure virgin comb.

> " Huge honeycombs of golden juice,
> Not only sweet, but fit for use."— VIRGIL.

This is a feat to be proud of, but years may elapse before such a result is attained, notwithstanding the devotion of unlimited time, and the exercise of special skill in fostering, which the many are not able to bestow.

An average price for a good swarm of English Bees, we may set down at 15s., a little more or less, according to the abundance of Bees in the neighbourhood. If we allow 2s. per annum for capital expended on a good frame hive, not a fancy article, and 3s. for sugar in hard times, we shall have an annual expenditure of 5s., and the stock, after the first year, may be fairly expected to return one swarm, value 15s., and say 20 pounds of honey, value 20s., a very large profit on the capital employed, setting aside exceptional years when two or more swarms will come off, or the exceptional harvest of 50 pounds or 100 pounds that, possibly, may gladden the eyes of the exultant Beemaster, also the contingency of the swarm in its first year, giving a surplus in honey or virgin swarm.

Is not this profit enough to satisfy all but the most grasping usurer? A labouring man residing in almost any rural district may keep quite fifty hives of Bees,

without interfering with his ordinary occupation; it is
not necessary that his own garden should contain them
all; the country clergyman or squire would, in nearly all
cases, obtain or give permission for the standing of hives
in their woods, fields, or waste grounds, and feel pleased
at being able to assist in the industry of their poorer
neighbours. The thousands of railway servants—station-
masters, porters, and signal-men—have splendid oppor-
tunities of increasing their incomes by Bee-keeping; the
Bees would prosper on, and gratefully accept the shelter
of, the railway banks, which are generally clothed with
flowers in all the luxuriance of their untended wildness;
and amongst the passengers using the stations would
be found willing customers for the honey and swarms.
Those who can make, buy, or borrow a "Honey Extractor,"
will derive a far larger profit, if using frame hives; and
such an instrument may be the joint stock property of a
whole village, travelling from one apiary to another. But
there is another kind of profit besides that of money.
Who but those who have experienced it can tell of the
large fund of instruction, pleasure, and amusement,
afforded by the busy Bees!

The industry and activity of Bees in their domestic
labours afford an instructive and amusing spectacle. All
are actively engaged; each attending, with all its power,
to the business to be done. Some feed the young larvæ,
others seal them over when full fed. A certain portion
attend upon the Queen; then there are the cell builders,
and the mighty moving army of honey and pollen
gatherers. No skulking, no idleness; each Bee knows
what it has to do and does it. Many employments are
there in the hive; some Bees ventilate, others perform all
the operations of scavengers, so that by night and by

day work goes on unceasingly in this busy home of
industry.

> "Behold' yon bord'ring fence of sallow trees
> Is fraught with flowers, the flowers are fraught with Bees;
> The busy Bees, with a soft murmuring strain,
> Invite to gentle sleep the labouring swain."—VIRGIL.

No need to stray from home in search of recreation in
our idle hours, the Bees will teach us these should be
unknown. Employment and interesting instruction will
always be found in the careful watching for the welfare
of the stocks in fine weather, and when the elements are
unpropitious our ideas may be enlarged and our me-
chanical genius fostered by the manufacture, improvement and invention of hives and appliances. In the
long evenings of winter all may be got ready for the
summer's requirements.

Many of our ablest Apiarians, whose means permit,
are content to sink pecuniary profit, and devote all their
energies to the philosophical study of the mysteries of
our industrious little friends and their works. Some
Bee-keepers also aim only at increase of Bees, finding
the sale of these pay better than honey; and, as a rule, it
may be taken as correct, that if the breeding power be
unduly pushed, the storage of honey must be sacrificed.

I will now suppose the reader is contemplating starting as a Bee-keeper. My advice is not to attempt too
much at first; begin in the spring with one or two
swarms; common Black Bees will do, though Ligurians
are better, if the additional cost be no object. Of the
former, a prime swarm should be obtainable for from
15s. to 20s., the Ligurians about double that price.

The inexperienced in Bee-keeping will do well when
starting, to buy in May, or the first half of June, a

swarm in preference to an old stock, unless he purchase of a person upon whom he can thoroughly depend.   There is always a chance of an old stock harbouring disease, especially foul-brood, a fatal disease which I will describe in good time ; which a novice would find impossible to eradicate.   A fair prime or first swarm will weigh net three and a half pounds ; a very good one, five pounds. They have been known to reach eight pounds. If lighter than three and a half pounds, they would probably be casts or second swarms.   These have the advantage, that the Queen is certainly young, and will probably become prolific, and are on this account not to be despised if they come early in the season.

Bees are usually sold in a straw skep, which will come in very handy, even if, as we should in this age of progression determine, to work with frame hives ; if this be not the case, and the straw skep is to be maintained, put the swarm on its stand at once, and leave it to proceed as Nature directs, not forgetting to protect it from the elements, and feed if necessary in bad weather (see " Feeding ").   If the swarm is to be transferred to a frame hive, see that the latter be ready, and find your instructions in the chapter on " Swarming."

If it be determined to commence with an old stock, a very good time to purchase is either in February, March, or April, thus gaining the advantage of the swarm when it comes.   In choosing an old stock, do not buy a weak one at any price; stand before the hives on a fine mild day and note those from which the Bees are busiest; buy such a one or none.

If the stock be bought within a mile or so of home, it should not be taken at once to its permanent resting-place, or the Bees on their next flight will most likely go back to their old quarters, and thus be lost to their purchaser; if possible, let it be removed at least two miles off, and remain there a week or ten days; after which, it may be brought home in safety. Evening should be chosen for the removal, or otherwise many may be abroad; but whenever it becomes a necessity that Bees should be removed during the day, administer a puff of smoke into the entrance of the hive. After this, those at home will be disinclined to go out, and in the course of half an hour all the Workers will have returned; the smoking should be repeated if it be found that the Bees are recovering from the sedative before the necessary time has expired. They should be moved or disturbed as little as possible in bad weather, for if they be excited and unable to take wing to relieve themselves within the next day or two, dysentery will very likely be engendered. The market value of a stock of Bees depends on their abundance in the neighbourhood, the season of the year, and the strength of the colony. Of course, in the autumn, when the dangers of the winter are all to come, they are not so valuable as in the spring, when they will, probably, soon swarm. Having bought an old stock, we have no option in the kind of hive to be used; whatever they are in must be made the best of, at any rate for a time. A novice could not satisfactorily transfer the Bees and combs while they are full of brood and honey, but if it be particularly wished to locate them in a frame hive, the transfer will become much easier 16 to 21 days after the issue of a swarm; at this time the combs are free, or nearly so, of brood. Supposing the old Queen laid on the day of her departure, her last Worker egg will be hatched in 21 days, and the young Queen has not yet or only just began to lay, the combs will, therefore, be light and manageable. The chapter on "Transferring" will give full instructions

E

how this operation may be successfully performed.   In settling the locality in the garden where the hives shall be placed, do not trouble about the aspect, it is immaterial, but seek if possible to place them where they may be sheltered from high winds and drifting rain. The shelter of a shrub or tree is very welcome, and they will be more likely to pursue their labours peacefully without annoyance to the frequenters of the garden; they are apt to be irritable if blown about by high winds. It is not material in which direction the hive is faced ; I have a partiality for East, as then the Bees get the morning sun, which is an advantage in winter.   When the afternoon sun shines full upon the hives the Bees are apt to be tempted out late, and get overtaken by the evening chill, which is death to them.

Hives should be sheltered from the full blaze of a midsummer sun ; but the whole of its grateful warmth should not be dispensed with, some heat being necessary to dry up moisture.   Perpetual shade is bad ; extremes either way should be avoided.   It is not advisable to crowd the stocks together; spread them about the garden singly, then the Bees will not be likely to fight, or the young Queens to get lost on their nuptial excursions.   Stands for the hives need not be expensive ; an old stool, box, cask, drain pipe, or log of wood, answers very well.   Should these look unsightly, climbing plants trained over will soon remedy that defect.   About 18 to 24 inches from the ground will be found a convenient height for manipulations.   The hives being disposed of in their permanent quarters, a careful study of the various chapters that follow will teach the tyro what to do and when to do it.   And, if attention be carefully bestowed, before the swarm multiplies itself or the winter arrives, the novice in Bee-keeping will find himself fully able to cope with any difficulties that may occur.

It has long been a debatable point whether Bees do best congregated in houses or standing singly about the garden ; of course, properly protected, the balance of opinion is for the latter course — mainly for two reasons. Firstly, the Bees are not so liable to rob and fight ; and a most important point, the young Queens, when returning from their matrimonial excursions, are not so likely to mistake the hive from which they issued—if they do, the penalty is *death*, for the Queen of the invaded hive allows no intruders. If Bee houses or sheds are used, they should be lofty enough for their owner to stand upright in for convenience in manipulation ; the hives should be far enough apart, at least three feet, and should be dissimilar in appearance. For hives made of thin material, like the Stewarton, shelter becomes a necessity, and indeed some Bee-masters obtain very successful results from Bees kept wholly indoors, egress and ingress being given to them by a covered way leading to the open air. I think a sound rainproof open barn or other building must prove a decided advantage, securing warmth and comfort. For three or four hives very pretty little Bee houses may be constructed, forming garden ornaments.

NATURAL SWARMING.

"Ten thousand pinions, guided by Thy hand,
Wander, unwearied, through the blue abyss,
They own Thy power—accomplish Thy command,
All gay with life, all eloquent with bliss!"——DERZHAZIN.

THE issue of a swarm of Bees in the bright and merry months of spring, is one of the most beautiful and de-lightful sights and sounds to be met with in the country side; everybody within view or hearing is attracted by the tumultuous assemblage, and if in a district where old customs are still rife, "tang-tang-tang" is heard on every side as the cottagers turn out with key and shovel to "ring the Bees." It is a popular idea that unless this is done the swarm will be likely to fly to a far distance, and perhaps be lost. I need hardly say the "ringing" has no effect whatever on the Bees, but the pleasant reminis-cences connected therewith make it always a welcome sound to hear.

Swarms do not usually issue until May or June, rarely in April. Early swarms are always desirable if the weather continue fine and warm, but if it be succeeded by cold or wet, then the early swarm becomes a misfor-tune; in the first place, the Bees have neither combs nor food, and being unable to go out foraging, must neces-sarily perish, unless fed regularly. The Mother hive also, lately so crowded, misses the comfortable warmth gener-ated by its departed population, and the Nurses with difficulty keep the temperature sufficiently high to mature the brood, so that in this contingency it will be seen it is more desirable for the swarm to issue later, when the weather can with more certainty be depended on.

Swarming is an act of necessity, not choice, and is a

provision of Nature to relieve an over-populated colony. It is in fact an emigration on a large scale.

Evidence in the minds of experienced Bee-keepers tends to prove, that the Queen in swarming is not a willing emigrant, but is forced to go out by the Workers.

First swarms usually come out in the middle of the day, and it must be fine and warm; but after swarms are very erratic; they may emerge early or late, in fair weather or foul, generally, however, in the former.

The chief indication that swarming is about to take place is the gathering of the Bees at the entrance of the hive, where they cling to each other and hang under the board in a cluster, often as large as a pottle measure. This clustering is evidently the natural instinct of the Bees, which leads them to gather together in the same manner as when they are making comb within the hive, and indeed they will sometimes start a new comb under the floor-board. The hive being quite full, the Bees will often thus "hang out" for two or three weeks, though something is apparently yet wanting to give them the final impulse to start. Clustering does not always take place before the issue of a swarm, so that other signs must also be watched for. If on one day the Drones are busy, and the Bees all activity and bustle, while on the following day few Bees are at work, and only a little restlessness observable, then we may probably expect a swarm at no very distant date; but there are no infallible signs by which the Apiarian can predict an immediate issue, more especially if it be a first.

The issue of after swarms may often be foretold by a shrill piping sound, to be heard in the interior of the hive, one or two days previously, the cause of which I will presently explain.

It is rarely that a first swarm will come forth in bad

weather; fine still days are generally selected, seldom earlier than nine or later than three o'clock, and most frequently between twelve and two.   As soon as the hive becomes inconveniently crowded, and Drones make their appearance, the Bees prepare for swarming by building a number of royal cells, and this having been done, the Bees' instinct soon teaches them it is time to form a new colony.   The first swarm is invariably accompanied by the old Queen, and she usually goes off as soon as one or more of the royal cells be sealed over; but even although the royal cells have arrived so far towards maturity, swarming may yet be stopped by unfavourable weather or other causes, in which case the embryo Queens will be destroyed.   Previous to swarming, her majesty becomes very restless, and instead of proceeding with her usual important business of egg-laying, roams restlessly over the combs.   Her agitation infects the whole colony; they rush to the honey cells, fill their honey bags, and fly in and out the hive as though impatient for the important event.   At length a violent commotion ensues; the Bees become almost frantic, whirling round in circles, continually enlarging, until at last the whole hive is in a state of the greatest ferment, and the Bees, rushing impetuously to the entrance, pour forth in one steady stream.

> " Upward they rise a dark continuous cloud,
> Of congregated myriads numberless,
> The rushing of whose wings is as the sound
> Of a broad river headlong in its course.
> Plunged from a mountain summit, or the roar
> Of a wild ocean in the autumn storm,
> Shattering its billows on a shore of rocks."—SOUTHEY.

It is generally supposed that the Queen leads the swarm, but this is not the case; she may come out with the first rush, or at any other time; as also on alighting she may be the first, or the cluster may form without her being there. If, however, she does not join soon, the Bees will scatter again and seek her. Often, when full of eggs, she is so heavy, that a long flight is impossible to her, and she falls to the ground, where the Bees will probably find her. Should the Queen be lost, the bereaved colony will exhibit the greatest agitation. Bees will be running about the entrance and up the sides of the hive searching everywhere for their beloved sovereign. This commotion is very noticeable the morning following the loss, while other colonies are quiet; after a day or two they become resigned. Once out, the Bees scatter themselves in the air like countless stars in the firmament; they dash hither and thither, whirling about with a pleasant noisy roar that may be heard at some distance; the whole atmosphere seems alive with Bees passing and repassing. They must now be attentively watched, when they will probably be found gradually converging together and settling down in one mass on some neighbouring bush or tree; although they will often, apparently not feeling satisfied with the home neighbourhood, fly far away, when the owner stands a good chance of losing them altogether. It is said that throwing up sand or dirt, flashing a mirror, or firing a gun amongst them, will often cause them to come down, but if these means fail, the owner has no resource but to keep his eyes and legs in the greatest activity, and follow the swarm until it settles. Seldom a neighbour will refuse a civil request to be allowed to enter his premises to reclaim an errant swarm, and the law of England is, that a right of property in Bees can be claimed so long as the swarm has been kept in sight, and the owner has the power to follow them on any man's land, with the proviso that compensation shall be made for any damage that he or his Bees occasion. Should the swarm be lost and no stranger hive them, they will often, after a few hours, return to their old hive, apparently disgusted at the neglect they have experienced. In this case, they may be expected to emerge again on the first favourable opportunity

In the case of a colony which will persist in repeatedly swarming, or if the Bee-keeper fears a swarm will issue and be lost, this may be prevented by clipping the Queen's wings; she may probably come out after this, but will be found not far away, as she, of course, would fall to the ground, her journey afterwards being limited to the distance she can crawl. This plan was known to Virgil, who says:—

> "The task is easy; but to clip the wings
> Of their high-flying arbitrary Kings."

The ancients styled the Queen—the King.

At the time of the old Queen's departure, the royal cells are generally arriving at maturity; in about a week one of them hatches, and the natural impulse of the new born Princess is to destroy all her unhatched sisters, in which she is assisted by the Workers; but if the hive be in that prosperous condition that another exodus is desirable, the Workers prevent this sororicide by setting a guard over the unhatched Queens; and when the reigning Queen approaches them she is driven unceremoniously back; she resents this interference by a quick succession of shrill angry sounds, not unlike the rapid utterance of *peep, peep, peep,* which is accepted by the imprisoned young Queens as a kind of challenge, and answered by them from the interior of their cells. This is called piping, and when heard is a sure sign of another swarm. The young Queens are all mature at the latest 16 days from the issue of the first swarm; and Langstroth says, if during this period these notes are not heard, it is an infallible indication that the first hatched Queen has no rivals, and that swarming is over for the season in that stock.

The second swarm usually issues on the second or third day after the piping is heard, though when the weather is unfavourable it may sometimes delay coming out until the fifth day. When using frame hives the issue of second and later swarms may always be prevented by destroying the Queen cells. Too frequent swarming is exceedingly injurious, as it leaves the original colony very weak, and the swarms are in the same condition; in fact, it divides a thriving stock into a number of weak ones, which, collectively, will not be so productive as one strong colony; therefore, unless under exceptional circumstances, after swarms should be discouraged. From a stock which swarms more than once no surplus honey can be expected, the largest returns of honey being from the hives which have not swarmed at all.

I will now suppose the swarm has issued, settled down, and all become quiet. The next thing to do is to hive it. Whatever hive is intended to become their permanent domicile, a straw skep is the best and handiest thing in which to bring home the Bees. Let the skep be clean and free from loose and ragged straws. If the Bees are intended to remain in it, see that the flight aperture is neatly cut, and the feeding hole well bunged up. Many persons run two sticks across the hive, at right angles to one another, to hold up the combs, and drench the inside of the hive with sugared water or beer, at the same time rubbing it round well with a bunch of sweet herbs. To the syrup I have no objection, although it is unnecessary; but the sticks and herbs are far better left out—the one becomes a nuisance in after manipulation, as well as causing crooked combs, and the herbs may not suit the organs of taste or smell of the Bees; that which we think is nice they may consider nasty. The floor board, which, of course, must be perfectly clean, is then placed handy on the ground, with a stout stick laid across a few inches from the alighting board; and duly equipped with veil and gloves, we are ready for operations. In all probability the swarm hangs on a bough or bush; in this case, all we have to do is to hold the hive fairly beneath and give the bough a vigorous shake, when the cluster will fall into the hive, and before the Bees can recover from their astonishment set it down on the floor board across the stick, which will tilt up the hive and prevent crushing; although, in inverting the hive on to the floor board, the Bees will fall on it, they will quickly run up again and cluster as before; and, provided the Queen be with them, every Bee outside will in a short time enter. If, on the contrary, the Queen be not shaken into the hive, it will quickly be deserted, and very likely the cluster will reform on the old spot, when the process must be repeated with, let us hope, a better result. It sometimes happens that when the Bees are apparently hived satisfactorily, they are not satisfied, but, issuing again, return to their old habitation or seek another home, when the same care in marking down and following must be pursued. Bees are not always so complaisant as to select a bush or bough to hang upon. The face of a brick wall is an awkward spot, and I have known them swarm upon that. The boll of a tree is a common place. In these cases they must be swept into the hive with a brush or goose's wing in the best manner possible under the circumstances; or the inverted hive may be supported

over them and the Bees driven upward with a little
smoke.   When in an awkward place, the Apiarian's
ingenuity must be exercised to devise the best manner
in which the desired object may be attained, bearing in
mind that Bees have a tendency to ascend, and may be
more easily driven or coaxed upwards than downwards.   A swarm should be hived as quietly as possible
after they have settled down, for if not secured within
an hour or two they will probably leave again.   After
being safely hived, and the stragglers gathered to the
main body, the stick may be taken away, and the new
colony placed at once on the stand it is to occupy.   If
this be not done *at once*, it will be better to leave it
quietly until evening, shading the hive from the sun's
heat by an umbrella or green boughs, as after the commotion of swarming has subsided, the industrious Workers, losing no time, will proceed to gather in some stores,
and on their return, not finding the hive, will perish.
The Bees forming a swarm always emigrate with their
honey-bags full.   They have provision enough to last
them three days; and if it be found at the expiration
of that time that the weather is unfavourable for work,
they must be fed, or if the famine continues they will die.
Driven Bees or forced swarms are not so full of honey,
and their wants must be attended to at an earlier period
in bad weather.   It should be remembered, as if written
in letters of gold, that Bees waste nothing, and so no loss
can occur by feeding them.   I cannot reiterate the fact
too often, that it is false economy to stint Bees in food;
they will not gather an ounce less of honey if they are
supplied with an unlimited amount of syrup; on the
contrary, the grateful nourishment will invigorate and
make them work still harder.   Should the Apiarian be
desirous of stocking a frame hive with the swarm, let it

remain quietly in the skep till five or six o'clock in the evening: then having the frame hive ready in the place it is to stand—all frames duly furnished with comb foundation or guide comb—remove the crown board or quilt, and carefully bringing the swarm to it, with a smart shake precipitate the whole of the Bees on to the top of the exposed frames—the major part of the Bees will quickly disappear downwards, and the remainder may be persuaded with a feather to follow, until there is not too many on top to allow the crown board or quilt to be replaced, when the work is done.

Another method is to spread a sheet or large newspaper on the ground near where the stock is to stand, and on it place the selected hive with its frames (which should have been previously furnished with guide combs) in position ; prop up the front an inch or so with a stick or stone, let the crown board remain on, then gently lift the skep, bringing it up to the frame hive, and with a quick, sharp jerk, shake the whole of the Bees on to the sheet immediately in front of the hive's entrance. The Bees will be so alarmed and terror-stricken at all the occurrences of this eventful day, that scarcely one will fly or sting, but make all possible haste to run under and up into the hive placed for them ; they may be assisted in this by gently sweeping them towards the entrance with a brush, stiff feather, or goose's wing. Search the skep well to make sure the Queen is not left behind, a few Worker Bees will not matter. It will soon be perceived, if the Bees are entering the hive quickly, if so, the Queen is there and all will go well ; but, if her majesty be absent, the Bees will crowd all about the outside of the hive, and although they may go in, they will not remain there. Finding this to be the case, we must seek an interview with her majesty, examine every little knot of Bees round about, for the Queen will seldom remain many minutes alone. Her faithful subjects crowd about, anxious for her safety, until a miniature swarm is formed, which, if not disturbed, will remain for days, until all the individuals composing it are dead of starvation and exposure. Should the Queen be found, introduce her to the hive, and it will then progress satisfactorily. After the Bees have all entered, gently lift up the hive, place it on its floor board, cover all up secure from cold and wet, and bearing in mind the caution as to feeding in bad weather, we may leave our young colony to fulfil its appointed task.

Should two or three swarms issue together or within a few hours, and the owner be not anxious to increase his stocks, these may be profitably amalgamated; three swarms put together will gather more honey than if kept separate. The best way to unite them is to hive them in separate skeps, and proceed as I have described for stocking a frame hive. It is advisable to well sprinkle each swarm with syrup, scented with peppermint, before uniting them; fighting will, by this precaution, not be likely to occur. If the Apiarian has no preference for either Queen, the Bees may be allowed to determine the right of sovereignty themselves; but if it be desired that a particular Queen should be the survivor, the others must be sought for and removed; this may be done by searching for the Queen when on the cloth, or in the skep, each lot separately, and not allowing the Workers to mingle until they be found. A Queen is very easily missed, and a tyro will, perhaps, find this a troublesome and difficult work.

The Bee-keeper is often sadly disappointed after all his trouble in hiving the swarm, to find in a day or two the Bees will not accept their quarters. Something is wrong about the hive which we cannot always define, and the swarm issues again ; in this case it is advisable at the next hiving to use another hive, for if you put them into the same as before, they probably will again desert it. When working with frame hives the swarm may almost always be induced to remain by giving them a comb of unsealed brood from another hive; the Bees cannot resist the temptation·to attend to the helpless young, and so remain. If the Queen should unfortunately have become lost, this brood will supply the Bees with the means of raising another.

If two swarms cluster together, they may advantage-ously be kept together, but if it be wished to separate them, the following plan may be pursued : Having hived the doubled swarm, drench them well with syrup from the rose of a watering-can ; then, having placed two other hives on a large sheet, shake down the Bees midway between them, and with a feather direct a stream of Bees towards the mouth of each; probably a Queen will go each way, but keep a sharp look out, and if you can capture both Queens, the process becomes simple. Give one to each hive, and with your feather arrange the stream of Bees so that they shall be about equally divided ; if one Queen only be captured, and the Bees are found quietly entering one of the hives, the other Queen is doubtless there ; but if the Bees are disin-clined to take possession of either domicile, then the Queen is still, probably, on the cloth, and the search must be continued.

Second and third swarms are led by Virgins, and if they issue when they are not wanted, they may be returned in the evening by shaking them out on a sheet before the entrance of the hive from which they issued, they will immediately run in ; it is advisable to remove the young Queen if possible before returning the Bees.

The increase of colonies by natural swarming requires the least amount of knowledge or skill, and will, with those Bee-keepers who have not acquired some degree of scientific Apiarian skill, be for long the only method allowed. Langstroth cites the following objections to natural swarming, which are, without doubt, well founded : "First. A serious objection to reliance on natural swarming, is the vexatious fact, that swarming hives are so constructed that although Bees often refuse to swarm at all, they cannot furnish to their crowded occupants sufficient accommodation for storing honey. Under such circumstances, hordes of useless consumers will often (for months) blacken the outside of the hives, to the great loss of their disappointed owners. Second. Another objection to natural swarming arises from the disheartening fact that Bees are liable to swarm so often, as to destroy the value of both parent stock, and its after swarms. Experienced Bee-keepers obviate this difficulty by making one good colony out of two second swarms, returning to the parent stock all after the second, and even that, if the season be far advanced. In frame hives, second swarming may be prevented by removing all the Queen cells but one; after the first swarm has left, by removing all but two; thus provision may be made for the issue of second swarms, if thought desirable, and yet all further swarming be prevented. After swarms, in many instances, have to be returned again and again before one Queen is allowed by the Bees to destroy the others. In this way a large portion of the gathering season is often wasted, as Bees seem unwilling to work with their wonted energy, so long as the pretentions of several rival Queens remain unsettled.

Third. Another very serious objection to natural swarming, as practised with common hives, is, that it furnishes no facilities for making vigorous stocks of late and small swarms. The time and money devoted to feeding small colonies are usually wasted, as the larger portion of them never survive the winter, and most of those that do are so enfeebled, as to be of little value. The more of such stocks a man has, the poorer he will be, for their weakness constantly tempts his strong stocks to plunder them.

ARTIFICIAL SWARMING.

To the perfection of methods of compelling Bees to swarm at will, Bee-masters have long devoted their attention, and the use of bar-frame hives offers great and valuable facilities for this purpose. How annoying it is, after having carefully watched a stock apparently ready to swarm for perhaps a week or two, when our attention has been unavoidably withdrawn for a time, to find that the Bees have issued and gone away, no one knows where. Apiarians engaged in business elsewhere than at home, have often but a poor chance of hiving their swarms; therefore, a knowledge of some means of artificial swarming is desirable. Straw skeps and frame hives require different procedure; for the latter there are several plans; for the former but one, which is *driving;* the method of this is explained in its proper chapter, therefore I will now merely point out when it may be resorted to. The most notable time is when the Bees hang out—this would not happen unless the hive were over-populated ; therefore, it is desirable to give immediate relief by driving, or what may be better called forcing a swarm. In driving for a swarm, a fine day must be chosen, and the driving performed as I have elsewhere given instructions. It is essential to consider whether the swarm is to be sent a distance away or to remain at home. A sufficient number of Bees should be driven into the empty skep *with the Queen* (*she being indispensable*), and in the first case we may nearly denude the old hive of the Bees, there will be quite enough abroad in the fields, who on their return home will furnish nurses for the brood, if the old stock be replaced on its former stand. The swarm should be at once tied up, and kept so until it reaches its new home. This mode of procedure cannot be adopted with safety if the stock and the swarm are to remain near together, as so many Bees would desert the swarm for their old home, that the new colony would, from want of strength, be practically useless. We may remedy this in various ways. The swarm may be temporarily sent away a distance of at least a mile and a half, and the old stock be replaced on its former stand ; the Bees which return home from the fields will then be found sufficient to carry on the work of the hive. After a few days the swarm may, after sunset, be brought back, when the Bees will have forgotten their old locality. Another and a very good way is to place the denuded hive on the stand of some other strong stock in the Apiary, removing that one a few yards away ; the returning Bees, although probably very much surprised at the new order of things in their home, will not hesitate to make the best of their misfortune, and proceed to hatch the brood and raise a Queen. In the swarming season the combs of a strong stock contain such an immense number of

F

young Bees, in all stages of development, that the hive soon becomes as populous as before.

If it is not convenient to adopt either of the above plans, then let only half the Bees, with the Queen, be driven from the old hive, and if the swarm be placed on the old stand its strength will be increased by desertions from the stock ; enough young Bees will be left in the latter to do the nursing.

The population will quickly be increased by hatching out, and if no Queen cells are in existence, the Bees will immediately start some, and a Queen will be hatched in from 10 to 16 days, according to the age of the larva or egg that has been converted from a Worker to a Queen. If the Apiarian can obtain a sealed Queen cell, or better still, a fertile Queen, supply the hive with it at once, taking proper precautions against the destruction of it by the Bees.   This will materially reduce the time during which the breeding ceases.

To a tyro, it is not easy to utilize surplus Queen cells in common straw hives. A few puffs of smoke blown into the entrance will so quiet the Bees that the hive may be turned up and examined, and Queen cells, being generally on the edge of the combs, are usually easily seen. If it be desired to remove one to another straw hive, it may be grafted into a like position it was removed from, or it may more advantageously be inserted at the top in the feeding hole, taking care the point of the cell be not obstructed, as from there the young Queen will make her entrance into the busy hive.   Once let the Bee-keeper master the art of driving, and he will no longer allow his Workers to hang out idle, or risk the loss of a swarm by waiting the pleasure of his Bees.

Where artificial swarming is carried on on a large

scale, Langstroth has devised an ingenious plan to re-populate denuded colonies:—

"Let the Apiarian obtain a forced swarm from some Bee-keeper a mile or two off. Bring it home and confine the Bees, allowing plenty of ventilation, until late in the afternoon or early next morning; then let him force four or five swarms, placing them at once on the stands of the parent stocks, and these latter where it is intended they shall permanently remain. The imported swarm should now be shaken out on a sheet and sprinkled with syrup, to prevent the Bees taking wing. With a saucer scoop up, without hurting any of them, as many Bees as you can, and carry them to the mouth of one of the old stocks from which you have driven a swarm; continue to do this until you have about equally apportioned the Bees. These Bees, having no previous home in your Apiary, will adhere to the different hives in which they are placed, and thus, without any further trouble, your parent stocks and forced swarms will alike prosper. If the Bee-keeper cannot conveniently obtain a swarm from a distance, he may use for this purpose the first natural swarm which comes off in his own Apiary, and by delaying to make artificial colonies until natural swarms begin to issue, every such swarm may be used for forming at least four artificial ones."

Dr. Donhoff gives a method to secure a colony which, when divided in the way above mentioned, will not forsake their new habitations:—

"On a fine evening, when the next day promises to be bright, drive out a swarm and set it in the place of the parent stock; next day, when it is warm, pour some honey amongst the Bees, and in a few hours they will swarm."

A forced swarm may also be made to take kindly to

their new quarters in the following way: Secure the Queen, and when the Bees show that they miss her, confine them to their hive (properly ventilated), until their agitation has reached its height. Then release them; and, as they begin to take wing, present to them their Queen, when they will cluster round her, and may be treated like a natural swarm.

I will now endeavour to describe the means by which advanced Apiarians form artificial swarms in frame hives. In the first place, if it be simply required to force a swarm for the purpose of supplying some one else with the Bees, we may adopt the following plan:—Remove the full hive ten or twelve yards away from its old stand, and, in its place, place the new hive which is to contain the swarm; then carefully remove and replace each comb seriatim from the old hive, and search for the Queen, who, being found, must be captured and carefully placed in the new hive, before which should be spread a sheet or broad board. Now take out the combs again, and, bringing each to the sheet, give it a sharp shake close to the hive, and the Bees covering them will be precipitated to the ground, and will immediately run into the entrance to rejoin their Queen. The hive should be propped up a little to give them easier access, and care should be taken that the sheet is so placed that the Bees cannot run under the *floor-board*.

When enough Bees are obtained to make a good swarm, they should be confined (with proper ventilation), removed where desired, and the first hive brought back to the old spot; or we may proceed as follows: Having a hive with frames of the same gauge as the one that is to supply the swarm, bring it to the side of the other, administer a puff or two of smoke, uncover, and when the crown board is removed, sprinkle the Bees with syrup. Now search for the comb on which the Queen is; having found it, transfer with any more frames of brood that can be spared to the new hive, and having put in their places the remaining frames, furnished with clean empty Worker combs, if possible, stand this hive in the situation of the full one; the returning Bees will people it and form a swarm. Another stand must be found for the old hive, a good many of whose Bees will desert it and tend to strengthen the new colony, headed by their old Queen, but enough will remain to carry on the business of the hive. We may often easily and economically make a new swarm by abstracting one or more combs of sealed brood, with all the Bees upon them, from a number of hives, putting all these into the new hive and confining them (properly ventilated) for a few days. Many of the bees even then will fly to their old home, but in their place others will have hatched. Before shutting them up, it is advisable to sprinkle them with a little scented syrup, or a fight might take place; but it does not often occur. Great care should be observed that no Queen is taken with the combs, or the strange Bees would probably kill her. The deprivation of one or two combs of brood will scarcely affect the old hives, if they are as strong as they should be; and if clean, empty combs be put in their places, the Queens will probably at once fill the cells with eggs. If any sealed Queen cells are known to be, or can be found, in any other hive, one may be given with advantage to each stock deprived of its Queen; time, which is all important at this season, is thus saved. By making one artificial swarm a week or ten days before the others, there may in the swarmed stock generally be found sufficient Queen cells to supply many hives; and in case a young Queen should emerge, she may be preserved from destruction by covering her with a cup Queen cage, or one of Mr. Carr's pattern.   Of course, it is preferable to supply the swarmed stock with a fertile Queen, if possible, as it must always be remembered that this saves one or two weeks of breeding time in the height of the season ; and as a young fertile Queen will lay 2000 or 3000 eggs per diem, the gain may be easily calculated.   In forcing swarms, be satisfied with one from each stock, or even two out of three ; prevent the issue, if necessary, of any more, and if the Bees have surplus energies, let them use them to gather honey, for it is a well-known axiom, that if many swarms are made there will be little honey ; the reason is obvious, the labour of the Bees is expended in nursing the young and providing them with sustenance, and this with a population constantly being reduced.

In removing frames from a hive, note should be taken of the order in which they are found, and they should be replaced in the same order, or they will not fit, and in some places the Bees will find no passage by which they can feed the brood.

HIVES.

"And, behold, there was a swarm of Bees and honey in the carcase of the lion."—JUDGES xiv. 8.

ONE of the primary considerations to the Bee-keeper is a proper selection of hives ; and in this chapter it is my purpose to give an impartial description of the most useful patterns with which I am acquainted.   It does not always follow that the most perfect hive is suitable to all ; in the first place, cost is ofttimes a great consideration.

One person will desire to study the natural history of the Bee, and use his Apiary very much for scientific investigation, without regard to pecuniary profit ; another will look to the latter point alone ; while a third will, perhaps, for want of leisure, or of education, only be able to manage the hive which gives the least possible trouble, content to sacrifice a large portion of profit. Hives naturally divide themselves into two great classes, viz. : straw skeps, where the combs are immoveable, and wooden frame hives, where the combs can be removed at will, and the whole internal economy of the hive investigated by the Bee-master. To the latter class of Bee-dwellings we are indebted for a great multitude of facts, which have in modern times come to light in Apiarian science, as well as many physiological discoveries, of great interest to the naturalist. The crude idea of moveable combs is, indeed, of very ancient date, having been adopted by the Greeks in the days of their prosperity, but having been of a very rude character, appear to have fallen into disuse ; the plan adopted was to induce the Bees to start their combs from moveable bars, but as they were generally attached to the sides of the hives, they required cutting away before removal, which in some measure prevented constant observation from the natural objection of the Bees to have their works destroyed. It was reserved for our own times to make a great stride in management by the invention of the moveable frames (in lieu of bars), suspended free in the hives, and removeable at pleasure without greatly disturbing the Bees. The credit of this device is attributable to the Rev. L. L. Langstroth, an American Bee-keeper of great renown, and another equally cele-brated German Bee-master named Dzeirzon, who seem simultaneously to have hit on the same plan, and who each constructed hives on this idea about the year 1851, which, with many slight modifications and improvements, form the governing principles of our most popular hives at the present day.

The use of straw skeps, as Bee dwellings, has been so long almost universal, that many Bee-masters have too often, without trial, condemned all other forms. The material of frame hives, *wood*, has been maligned times without number, as an encouragement to damp, and all manner of evils have been predicted for the unfortunate Bees, compelled to dwell in a wooden domicile. The prejudice is now gradually dying away, until we find all those, who are for progression, giving in their adherence to the oft-proved fact, that the frame hive gives the best results, when managed with ordinary care. By the use of moveable frames, we can at all times make ourselves acquainted with the exact state of our colonies—equalize by exchange of combs their stores and brood ; weak colonies may be strengthened, or united to others without trouble ; swarms made when desired, saving all care and anxiety of watching ; and, to an almost certainty, swarms may be prevented when supers are required to be filled. Feeding may be conducted in a clean and efficient manner, and the wonderful doings of the Bees are at all times open to the discerning eye of the student. Other objections to frame hives are, that they are costly, and require the expenditure of too much time. The cost of a frame hive is entirely optional. I hope presently to show, how the poor man may find it scarcely exceeds that of a skep, with its floor-board and cover, and for the trouble, whatever time is given in excess of that bestowed on a straw skep, will be amply repaid. In America many men keep bees as a trade, and there the labour of one man is sufficient for 150 or

200 hives, and unless he employs his spare time in manufacturing his hives and appliances, he finds six months of the year at least with nothing to do. If I except about ten weeks in the midst of summer, when swarming and honey gathering is in full progress, I am at a loss to know how any man, with a dozen frame hives, could usefully bestow on them an average of an hour's labour a week; he may spend, in season, any amount of time in studying and watching his little favourites, but this would be of more advantage to himself than the Bees. In fine summer weather I rarely commence my daily duties without spending half an hour with my Bees, and this short interval is certainly the most enjoyable of the day. An advocate for straw skeps, in pitting the weight of his honey crop against that from a frame hive, too often forgets to take into consideration, *quality*—the bruised and broken combs, the discoloured run-honey, frequently adulterated with all the impurities of the hive, that would pass through the strainer, can no more be fairly compared to the spotless purity of the well-filled combs of the frame supers, than can the strawberries of the woods be compared to the large luscious fruit of the gardens. If the Bee-keeper be content to let the Bees manage themselves, without ever intending to afford them any assistance, then it is quite immaterial whether straw skeps or frame hives be used; but if it be desired to obtain all advantages possible from the Bees, then adopt the best aids for this purpose—*frame hives.*

I commence with a description of

STRAW SKEPS—The general form of which is known to all. These, although fast being superseded, are yet used, and will be for many years to come the common hives of the cottager. I will endeavour to point out the best varieties. Now, the straw skep, although very far from the *best* hive, is not to be despised; indeed, it is a very useful hive, and however advanced the Bee-keeper may be, generally, he is not wholly without it in one pattern or the other. If a census were taken of the Bees' dwellings throughout Britain, the skeps would far outnumber all other kinds put together. A well-made straw hive is warm and healthy for the Bees, and cheap to their owner; indeed, most cottagers make their own, costing almost nil, and affording employment for a wet winter's day when other work is scarce. I like a skep, it is so nice and handy; and if its interior were not like a sealed book it should have an honoured place in my Apiary; but its great disadvantage is the impossibility of investigating its internal economy with satisfaction.

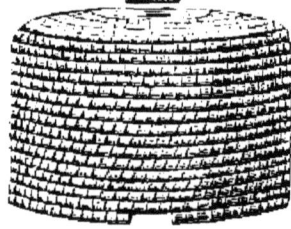

Fig. 4.   Fig. 5.

COMMON COTTAGE STRAW SKEP.—Two patterns are generally followed in making these hives. The one which I suppose we may call the "original," Fig. 4, a closed dome, usually with a ring at the top; the other the "improved," Fig. 5, has a flat top, with a feeding hole in the centre, which should not exceed two inches in diameter. This latter is incomparably the best, as it affords proper facilities for feeding the Bees, which will often save their lives; its cost is from 1s. to 4s. 6d., and it may be purchased in most country towns. All straw

hives are much improved and their durability increased
by encircling their bases with a flat wooden hoop 2 or
2½ inches broad. The hive known as the "Pettigrew
Hive" is nothing more than a large flat-topped skep.
There are three sizes, viz., 16-inch, 18-inch, and 20-
inch in diameter, that is their width inside measure, and
12 or 14 inches deep. When well filled they weigh
respectively 60 pounds, 100 pounds, and 130 pounds.
They are made in Ayrshire of wheaten straw, neatly and
firmly built. These hives are largely used in the North
of England and in Scotland; and Mr. Pettigrew quotes
instances where the Bees have in them gathered as
much as 164 pounds gross weight of contents. When
using such large skeps the Bees cannot be expected
to store any honey in supers, and in a great measure the
quality of the honey is sacrificed without any adequate
benefit. The combs in the main hive must of necessity
become soiled from the labours of the immense population; while, had half the store been gathered in supers,
this half would be worth as much as double the quantity
from the breeding hive. To those who determine on
the use of straw skeps I would recommend the pattern
of Fig. 5, of about 14 inches in diameter by 8 inches deep,
inside measure. These will be found a very manageable
size, admitting the use of a super when required. For
exceptionally good localities larger hives may be used.
It is highly important that the material of which they
are made should be good sound straw, and the bands of
adequate thickness; for on this, be it remembered, depends in a great measure the well-doing of the stock.
Each hive will require a sound wooden floor-board—if
1½ or 2 inches thick, so much the better. In country
districts these are well and economically cut out of the
boll of a felled tree. It should be at least 1 inch greater

in diameter than the hive, and have a projecting front for the Bees to alight on (see the floor-board on Fig. 10), which should, with the remainder of the margin of the board, be bevelled off for the rain to run off.   However well the skep may be made, it would be folly to expose them to the weather without protection from the rain, and many plans may be adopted to guard against this. A very rural way is to make a conical straw hackle, Fig.

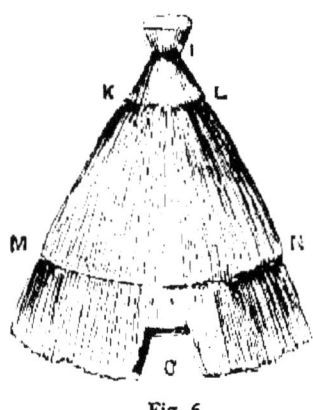

Fig. 6.

6, fitting over the hive, and throwing off the water like the thatch of a barn. Another way is to cover the hive with an inverted flat milk pan, such as is used in dairies to set the milk in. It matters little what is used so that the desired result be obtained, for it must be borne in mind that a dry hive in winter is one of the first essentials for prosperity.

The straw hackle, Fig. 6, can be made without difficulty, thus : The straw having been well soaked, as for thatching, is securely tied with basket-maker's twigs or tarred string.   Hoops are then fastened within at K, L, and M, N.   The hackles are then fitted over and adapted to the form of the hives, then left to dry, stiffen, and set. A wooden peg or two passed through the hackle above the hoop into the hive side will prevent the wind disturbing it.

The following suggestions, published in 'The Country,' by Mr. Cheshire, for skep covers will be found both useful and ingenious :—

"Double back upon itself a flour or manure sack, as

you would a stocking before putting it on, and draw this down over the skep until the doubled edge is round the lower part of the hive, just above the flight hole, which should be kept open by a little bridge of wood, zinc, or tin. A cord may now be tied round the sack at the lower part, while shavings, sawdust, or straw should be filled in between the parts of the sack, as it were between the foot and leg of the stocking, until the hive crown is well covered, for here it is that the loss of heat is the greatest. The sack's mouth being tied, the operation is complete, and we may make the hive sufficiently secure to winter in the open by putting over it an inverted milk-pan, if of sufficient size, or, better, the cover, Fig. 9, to be presently described. I could wish all skeps were too large to be covered by American cheese-boxes; but this not being the fact, I will explain how these covers, which may be obtained for the sum of 3d., may be made into capital rain-tight protectors, good for ten years' wear. The lid of the box, placed on four inverted flower-pots, or some bricks, will make an excellent bottom board, while the box proper forms the case for the hive itself. Before being used, the bottom of it, which will be its top as a hive case, should be painted well over with hot pitch, which should be made to cover 1 or 2 inches down the side. A sheet of newspaper, or canvas if preferred, should now be evenly spread over the cold pitch, when, by the application of a hot flat iron, used after the manner of the laundress, the pitch is remelted, well incorporated both with the wood and the paper, all cracks are closed, and the cover made absolutely rain-proof. The box may now be placed over the hive, which should be previously furnished with sufficient hay, straw, sacking, or such like material, to fill up any spaces. A capital cover may be made of roofing-felt, which is sold for 8d. the yard run, and is 2 feet 8 inches wide. It should be cut as

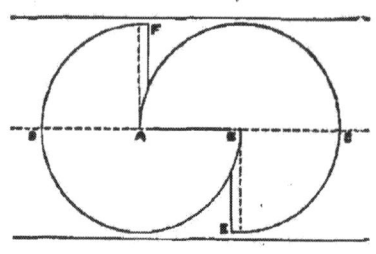

Fig. 7.

shown in Fig. 7. Make a notch in a lath, 17 inches from its end, at 1 inch from which bore a hole with a brad-awl, which stick 16 inches from the end of the felt at B, and equally distant—that is, 16 inches —from each edge. With chalk in the notch in the lath run round the three-quarter circle, A, C, E. Now place the awl at A, and describe the three-quarter circle F, D, B. Cut out the two covers through F, A, B, E. Draw their straight edges together, until one edge touches the dotted line. Tack these two edges together into a thin lath, and the cover is in form. The waste pieces of felt, which will be very small, will suffice for four straps, to be fastened underneath by clenched nails, and which may

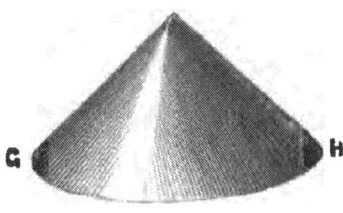

Fig. 8.

be tied to the hive by a string passing round it. This will effectually prevent the cover being blown away in the stiffest gales. Fig. 8 shows the cover complete; it will be 24 inches in diameter, G, H, and will

afford, in consequence of its greater size, far better protection than a milk-pan, while it costs only 5½d. Coated with tar, and afterwards sprinkled with hot sand, this cover will last many years. The same form in zinc would be more sightly, but it would cost about 1s. 6d. for material."

NEIGHBOUR'S IMPROVED COTTAGE HIVE.—This has

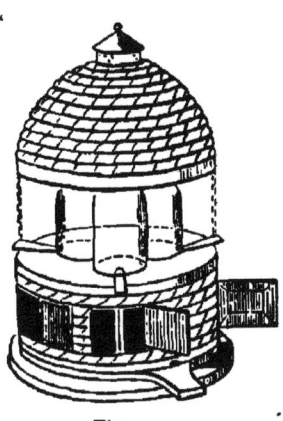

been a popular hive for many years, and is pretty and interesting to those who are satisfied with an imperfect view of their industrious labourers. It consists of a circular straw lower compartment, or main body of the hive, having three windows with outside shutters. A thermometer is fixed across the centre window, so that the Bees cannot work between it and the glass, and thus intercept the view of the graduated scale.

Fig. 9.

The stock hive, encircled with a hoop, rests on a stout floor-board, fashioned with a projecting landing-place for the Bees. The top is also of wood, having three or more circular openings of about 3 inches in diameter, to receive as many bell-glasses, having fixed on their tops internally a tube of perforated zinc for ventilation, to which guide-combs may be fastened, and which also forms a convenient support for the Bees when commencing their labours; over all is fitted a cover of straw (also hoop-bound), closely fitting the top of the stock hive, and permitting removal with great facility to allow inspection of operations; this straw cover is surmounted by a ventilator forming a neat finish. The price of this, 35*s.*, is, however, a bar to its general use, more especially as, unlike most hives of an equal cost, the combs are immoveable.

EKES AND NADIRS.—An eke is an additional space added on to a hive *below* the original. They are principally used with straw skeps, when the Bees are pressed for room; the hive is lifted up, and a ring like the rim of a sieve, in either straw or wood, placed on the floor-board and the hive placed on it; the Bees will then continue their combs downwards, and will usually not swarm. If more room is still required, add another eke. When full, the ekes may be severed from the main hive by a wire, but the honeycomb in them will only be fit for run-honey, as it will be contaminated with brood and Bee-bread. The straw-hivists, who boast of their 160 pounds of contents in a straw hive, reckon the ekes as a part of the hive; in the rare case of this extreme weight being attained, one-third at least would be dross.

A nadir is another complete but empty hive, with open feed-hole, placed below an over full one, where the Bees have been hanging out. These should be cemented together at the junction, and the Bees will then go down through the feed-hole, and fill the lower hive with combs in which the Queen will breed; the upper hive may at the end of the season be removed, and the combs cut out for run-honey. The only advantage, and that is a doubtful one, I can see in nadirs is, that the Bees get new combs for old ones, and swarming is prevented, if undesirable. Neither ekes nor nadirs are much used in the South of England.

FRAME HIVES.—When my opinion is asked, what hives I recommend for use, I say without hesitation FRAME HIVES; but if the interrogation proceeds further, and I am asked what particular hive, I answer, I advocate the principle only. It matters little to the Bees, or the profit they will produce, whether the hive is made of the finest mahogany or the commonest deal; and nine-tenths of the little absurd intricacies which hive-makers delight to furnish their hives with serve but to increase expense, and confuse the unfortunate tyro in Bee-keeping. When I have examined minutely and *seriatim* the large collection of hives at a great Bee Show, I have been often struck with the many eccentricities, called "inventions," which their owners doubtless honestly believe will tend to benefit Apiculture, but which an experienced impartial person condemns at once as useless. In my own Apiary I have hives of several patterns, and among them all I greatly prefer the hive for which Mr. Cheshire obtained the principal prize at the first Crystal Palace Show. This has the great merit of simplicity, combined with working facilities and sound principles of construction. A well-made hive, all parts accurately fitting, affords a good deal of ease and comfort to the manipulator; but to the Bees themselves, the hive of the rudest, roughest construction, provided it be weather-proof, is just as good as the work of the most experienced joiner, and the skilful Bee-master, I have no doubt, can obtain as good results from the first as the last. There are probably some hundreds of varieties of hives, each in some one's opinion surpassing all others; it is, therefore, in vain for me to think of indicating "the best," so I will content myself with describing some of "the best" in such a manner as will, I hope, enable the poor man to make his own at little cost, and the rich man to purchase a satisfactory dwelling for his Bees.

As with the hives, so with the frames. Discussion both here and in America has waxed hot and fierce as to their form and size. The only essential requirements are, that they shall be of such a width as shall allow $1\frac{1}{2}$ inches from centre to centre, when in position in the hive. Their length and depth may vary at the owner's pleasure, provided that all in the same Apiary are exactly the same size, so as to be interchangeable. It is reasonable to suppose, that localities that produce much honey will fill larger combs than poorer places, and therefore it is impossible to fix a standard size for all. Several hive-makers are advertising "standard hives" and "standard frames." They may be their standards, but for general use they are nothing of the kind. In England, probably the Woodbury frame is more generally used than any other, and we may seek far before we find a better. In the United States, many frames are in use. The following is a diagram of the principal, of which the Langstroth seems to be the favourite; but for English use, excepting very favourable localities, this is perhaps too large:

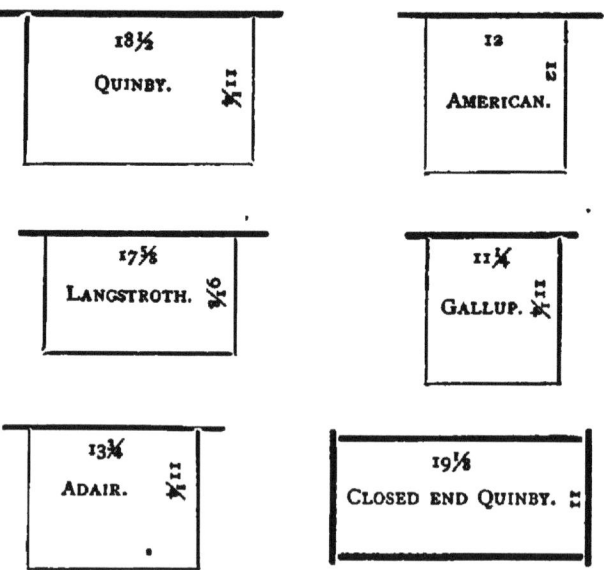

The balance of opinion seems to be, that shallow frames are better for use than deeper ones.

THE CHESHIRE CRYSTAL PALACE PRIZE HIVE. —

Fig. 10.

The Judges at the first Great Apiarian Exhibition, after having examined the many hives shown, awarded the palm to Mr Cheshire for this hive; and, as I have before intimated, I quite concur in their judgment, and those who can afford its purchase will find it easy to work with, giving the minimum of disturbance to the Bees, as well as affording every facility to investigate all parts. I extract the following description from the pages of ' The Country' :—

" The hive consists of two main portions; the super cover, and the hive proper, the lower portion in which breeding is carried on. Over the entrance is a porch. This is chamfered off towards the end, the more

effectually to carry away drip, and has a channel near
its front edge, which acts as a gutter, by which the
rain is conveyed to its ends. This gutter is shown in
the cross section, Fig. 11, at E. The bottom-board
of the hive projects $2\frac{1}{2}$ inches along the front, so as to
form a very convenient alighting board. The flight-hole
is 10 inches in length, and is formed by cutting from the
hive-wall a piece a full $\frac{1}{4}$ inch deep (see G, Fig. 11). F,
Fig. 11, is screwed on beneath the porch roof to give it
additional stability, and also to provide the groove for
two sliding shutters (shown in Fig. 11), by which the
entrance way may be regulated as occasion may require.

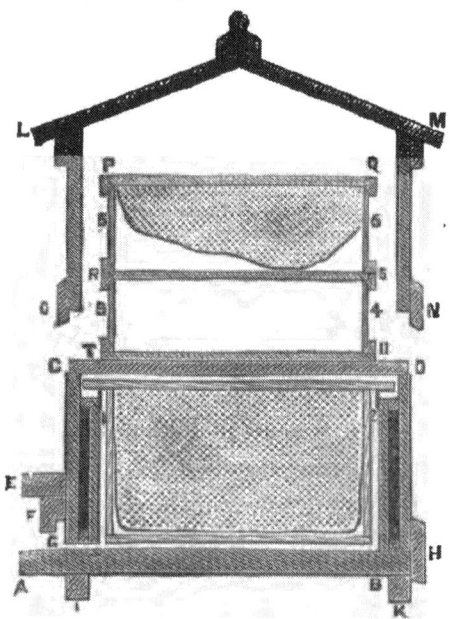

Fig. 11.

Upon the upper part of the ends of these are two small
studs preventing the shutters from meeting, so that the
entrance can only be reduced to about half an inch.

This arrangement prevents the accidental closing of the hive mouth to the destruction of the colony, while it admits of its (*i. e.* the mouth's) immediate lessening in the event of robbing, or for the purpose of wintering. Should, however, the absolute stopping of the entrance way be desired, the doors may be removed, and put in, the right on the left, and the left on the right, when they will meet, as their studs will be on their outer instead of their proximate ends.

"The bottom-board is so contrived that it can be removed without disturbing the Bees, as it slides upon two runners seen beneath it in Fig. 10. Blocks I and K, Fig. 11, fitted in between these runners and bottom-board, press it against the hive body and hold it in position. The legs are fastened to the hive proper, so that it carries its own stand. When the bottom-board is slipped into position it is stopped by a back piece, H, Fig. 11. The super cover, the upper part of Fig. 10, or L, M, N, O, Fig. 11, is hinged, and so contrived by the aid of a chain that it can only open until its lines, horizontal when *in situ*, become perpendicular, and *vice versa*. The advantage this supplies beyond the ordinary loose case is considerable. It is sometimes inconvenient to find suitable standing for the latter during manipulation, while this arrangement provides the Bee-master with a table, often of great service when the hive is open, upon which he can place his smoker, syrup, knife, &c., during his operations.

"The walls of the hive are double, as may be seen by reference to Fig. 11, and have between them a space containing dead air, shown by the black broad lines.

"The dummy (*h, i*, Fig. 12), which usually hangs next the hive side, and gives play to the combs by its removal, is simply a double board the same size as a frame.

"In order to give room for the ears of the frames, the inner skin, front and back, is made an inch shallower than the outer one. Standing 3-8ths of an inch above the former are two strips of zinc (1 and 2, Fig. 11), each about an inch wide, and which serve to carry the frames so that they cannot be propolised, while they—*i. e.* the frames—can be slidden backwards and forwards with the greatest ease during manipulation. The top bar of the frame is 3-8ths thick, so that the space between the top bar and the cover is $\frac{1}{4}$ inch. The depth of the hive (D, H, Fig. 11) is $8\frac{3}{4}$ inches, the width within between 1 and 2, $14\frac{1}{2}$ inches, the frames being exactly the same in size as those known as Woodbury's. The length (C, D, Fig. 11) will vary with the number of frames used, but 11 seems to give the hive the correct capacity.

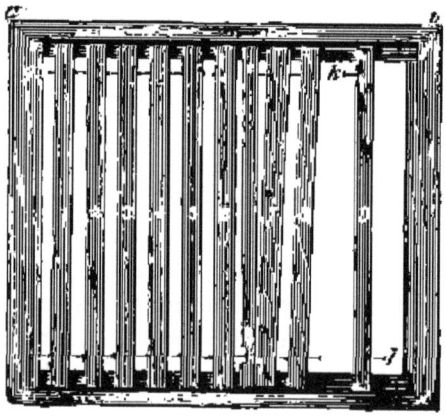

Fig. 12.

"Fig. 12 shows the arrangement of the frames, which are kept at their correct and relative distances by means of small nails known amongst carpenters as panel pins. Combs 1 to 6 are shown *in situ*, and by having the dummy, as in the figure, a small swarm,

instead of weakening itself by excessive distribu tion
would be cosily confined to about half the hive; and in
some cases it might be an economy of heat, and in other
ways advantageous to still further reduce their working
space.   It is here worthy of remark that, removing the
dummy from the end of the hive beyond frame 11,
where it would usually remain, and placing it in any
part, does not prevent the 11 frames being accommo-
dated as before, for if the dummy stands, as in the figure,
outside No. 6, the frame beyond it—*i. e.* No. 7—will
touch the dummy at one of its ends, and so give space
for the full length of the distance pin of the last frame.

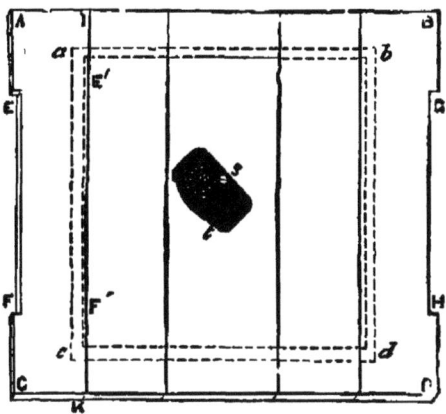

Fig. 13.

" Fig. 13 represents the crown-board, the edge of
which is seen at C, D (Fig. 11).   This consists of five
strips or slats, clamped at their ends to prevent warping;
they are each 17½ inches long.

" The width of the central strip is 5 inches, while that
of the others is 3¾ inches.   The central one is pierced
with a hole 1½ inches in diameter, and over this is placed
a feeding stage.   At E, F, and G, H, the top board is

cut away $\frac{1}{4}$ inch in width and 10 inches in length. Notwithstanding the removal of these parts, the board completely covers the hive top, but if the outside slat (A, I, C, K) be made to change places with the one next it, E, F will occupy the position E', F', and will form a long hole or slat, which will give the Bees ingress to the super, the frame of which occupies the position of the dotted lines, *a, b, c, d.* The same being done on the other side, the Bees are freely admitted to the super, while the Queen, the Nurses, and the pollen gatherers of the brood nest beneath are prevented by an unbroken ceiling from passing up into and spoiling the honeycomb in the super."

This hive is made by Lee, of Bagshot, and sold at 23*s.* to 35*s.*, according to completeness and workmanship.

WOODBURY HIVE.—This hive with which the late

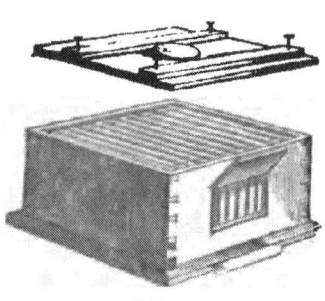

Fig. 14.

Mr. Woodbury, of Exeter, introduced the bar-frame system was, I believe, first described by him in the 'Journal of Horticulture' (to which he was a leading contributor), in 1861. Although some improvements have been made, which I will presently endeavour to describe, the term "Woodbury Hive" is still a household word amongst Bee-keepers, and there are few of any note who have not partly or wholly adopted it at one time or another.

The following is Mr. Woodbury's own description of a ten-frame hive, as it appeared in the 'Journal of Horticulture':—

"Frame hives are made of inch wood, 14$\frac{1}{2}$ inches square, and 9 inches deep inside, dovetailed and put together with paint, the ends of the dovetails being pinned through with stout iron wire driven from the top and bottom, and meeting in the centre. A window $7\frac{1}{2}$ inches long by 4 deep affords a slight view of the interior from the back (not the front, as engraved), but is much obstructed by the frames. The crown board which is raised in the engraving (Fig. 14) is keyed to prevent warping, and is secured by four long brass screws passing through the ends of the keys. A 2-inch central hole for feeding is the only aperture, and this is closed when not in use by a circular block of $1\frac{1}{4}$-inch wood, 5 inches in diameter. A 3-8th rabbet is cut out of the top inner edge at the back and front, and below this are notches 7-8ths wide by 3-8ths deep, in which rest the ends of the frames. This arrangement affords the Bees a free passage above the frames, as well as below at their sides. The annexed sketch (Fig. 15) of the interior angle of the hive is drawn the full size, and will serve as a guide for the arrangement of the frames.

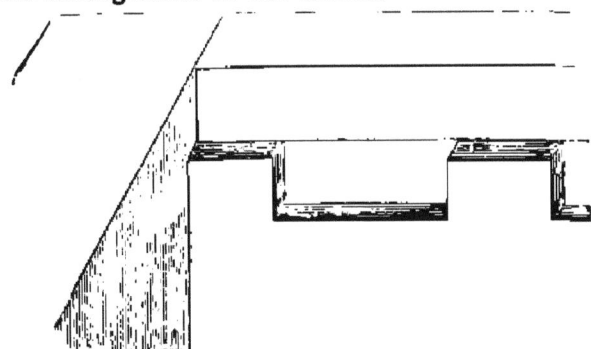

Fig. 15.

" The slips of wood forming the frame are 7-8ths of an inch wide, and 3-8ths of an inch thick ; and the projections at the top are 5-8ths of an inch long. When in its place the whole forms a frame 13 inches long by $7\frac{1}{4}$

inches high (inside measure), with a 5-8th projection at each end, which rests in its appropriate notch in either

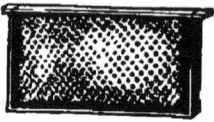

Fig. 16.

the back or front of the hive. The accompanying engraving (Fig. 16) represents the frame filled with comb, in which state the comb becomes so firmly cemented to the frame as to admit of its being handled with the greatest facility."

This, which we may call the father of our frame hives, although very good, has shown sundry inconveniences easily remedied. In the first place the crown-board, although "keyed," is very liable to warp, and thus gives the Bees more air than is at all times desirable; again, when firmly propolized down by the Bees it was difficult to move without a great shock and irritation to them, so now it is usual to make the crown-board in three or four pieces (strips), and not screw them down at all. The Bees will soon make them fast, and indeed ofttimes too fast; then one piece at a time can be removed, thus exposing but a small surface of the hive's interior if desired, and a small piece of wood of course is more easily detached from the propolis adhesion than a large one. The notches forming resting-places for the ends of the frames have often been found a great nuisance; the Bees, who are careful architects, will insist on firmly fixing each bar in its place; and where removal is frequently desired, considerable trouble occurs in detaching them, the small dividing blocks between the notches often breaking away, until three or four are run together. This inconvenience may be obviated by reducing the height of back and front to 8½ inches, and instead of the notches to form one plain rabbet, in which the frames are placed; but here we must have some contrivance to keep them a proper distance apart. One of the most useful is to drive a stout wire pin or French wire nail into the side of the frame, about $\frac{1}{2}$ an inch from the ends, projecting just far enough (about 19-32nds of an inch) to keep them at proper distance; two on each frame will be found sufficient, one at the top left side, the other at the bottom right side, with a similar peg in the left side of the hive *front*, and ditto right side *back*. These hives are sold at various prices, from about 8*s*. to 25*s*., according to workmanship and completeness, with stand cover, supers, &c.

THE COTTAGE FRAME HIVE.

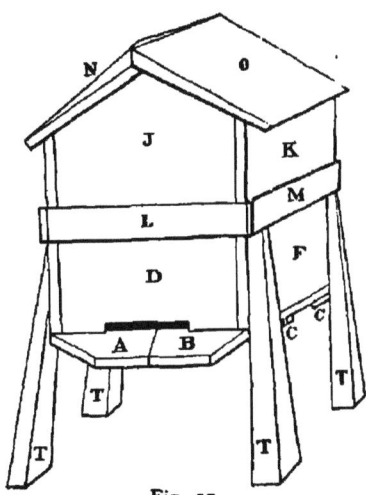

Fig. 17.

Very often when I have recommended labouring men to make their frame hives themselves, and referred them to printed descriptions, I have been met with the reply that they cannot work from description, but if they could have a pattern they could accomplish the work. It is impossible to distribute far and wide, as I should like, pattern hives without great cost; but I here endeavour, as the next best plan, to give drawings and dimensions of every piece of wood requisite for a good cottage frame hive. My aim is to describe the simplest and least expensive method of hive-making. Hammer, saw, and plane are all the tools absolutely necessary, and these most people can use with skill enough to make a hive such as I describe, that with ordinary care will be found serviceable twenty years hence. Let me say perfection is not aimed at, but simply such a hive as will carry out the main principles of modern rational Bee-keeping, and be infinitely better than the closed straw skeps of our forefathers. I hope my instructions will be found simple enough to enable every poor man to set up a serviceable frame hive. The "Woodbury" size is very convenient, and with many modifications, which have all been before adopted, I shall follow its design.

When we build a house we commence with the base-

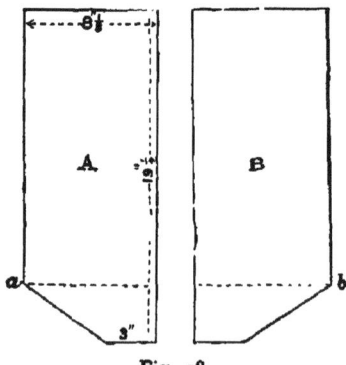

Fig. 18.

ment, and so we will do the same with our hive and proceed to describe the floor-board. Cut two pieces of wood 1 inch thick, the shape and dimensions of A and B. Rule a pencil-line from a to b, and bevel off the part below it to half the thickness of the wood to form a slope for the rain to run off; then bring the two inner edges together, and prepare two battens, as C, of

unplaned wood, which nail or screw crosswise underneath about 3½ inches from each

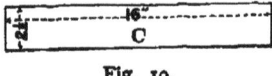

Fig. 19.

end. The floor-board should be fastened to the body with screws. This being complete, I proceed to describe

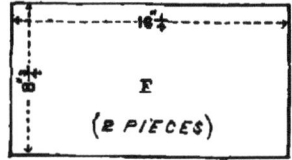

Fig. 20.

the hive-body. This is simply a bottomless and topless box made of inch deal, 14½ inches square by 8¾ inches deep inside measure. Two pieces of wood, as F, will form the sides, and for the back and front cut two more pieces of the shape and dimensions of D and E, which having planed

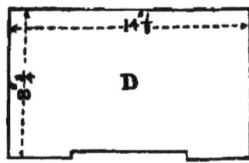

Fig. 21.

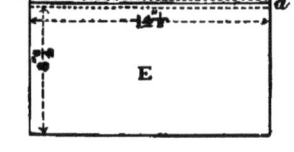

Fig. 22.

on one side as the others, with a rabbet-plane or tenon-saw cut out from the unplaned side of one of the long edges of D and E, a rabbet 1⅛ inch deep, and half the thickness of the wood, as at E. Procure two strips of zinc, 14½ by 1 inch, and fasten these with tin tacks over the angle *a*, as shown by the dotted lines, so that the upper edge of the zinc shall be exactly 5-8ths of an inch lower than the top edge of the wood; now nail these four pieces of wood together, D and E inside the F's, and the hive-body will be complete. The crown-board will be composed of the five pieces G (2), H (2) and I,

Fig. 23.

Fig. 24.

also of 1-inch wood; these, placed side by side, with the irregular edge of G outwards, in the order of G, H, I, H, G, will cover the top. It will be perceived that I

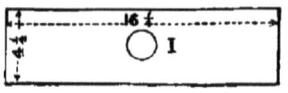

Fig. 25.

has a circular hole $1\frac{1}{2}$ inch diameter, cut clean through the wood, for use in feeding. When access to a super is required to be given to the Bees, it is only necessary to reverse the pieces G, placing the slit inwards; the five parts of the crown-board will not require joining together, being handier separate, they do not cast so readily, and a portion of the hive can be uncovered at a time, without unnecessarily exposing the whole surface.

Of vast advantage to perfect Bee-keeping is an upper chamber to the hive, within which supers may be placed and feeding carried on undisturbed by Robber Bees.

J, K, L and M, two of each, will form this, and will

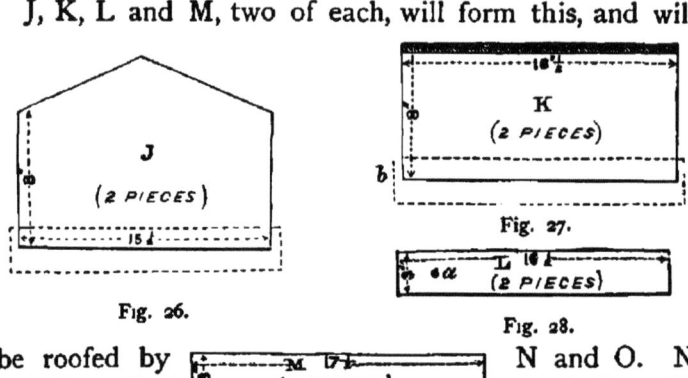

Fig. 26.

Fig. 27.

Fig. 28.

be roofed by

must be nailed

and the upper

Fig. 29.

N and O. N on before O, edge, as also

the outer upper edge of the sides K, must be bevelled off

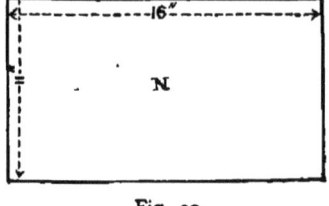

Fig. 30.

at such an angle as will allow O to lie flat, as in the figure of the complete hive. The fillets, L, M, must be nailed on J, K, as in the dotted lines b, $1\frac{1}{4}$ inch on, and the same below, when the upper story should fit easily over the hive-body, the fillet keeping it securely in place. All these pieces should be made of ¾-inch wood (excepting L and M, which should be ½-inch), planed on one side. It will be found

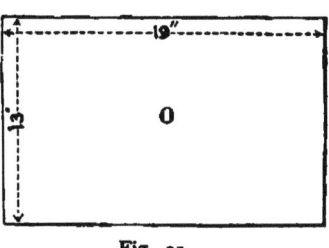

Fig. 31.

very convenient to have fixed on at the left side a pair of hinges, one flange screwed on the under edge of the fillet, the other on the hive's side beneath; and on the back fillet at *a*, and on the back of the hive-body 3½ inches below that point, screw in an iron ring, and connect these two rings together with 27 inches of chain or cord, which will permit the hive cover to be raised without removal from the hive; it will be found a great convenience.

The whole externally should now be well painted with three or four coats of light-coloured paint, and will then be ready for furnishing with the frames. Slips of

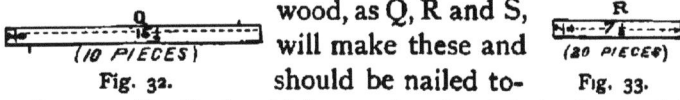

Fig. 32.   Fig. 33.

wood, as Q, R and S, will make these and should be nailed together as P: Q should be made of 3-8th-inch wood, R and S of ¼-inch, and they need not be planed. Now having at hand some bell-staples or French wire-nails,

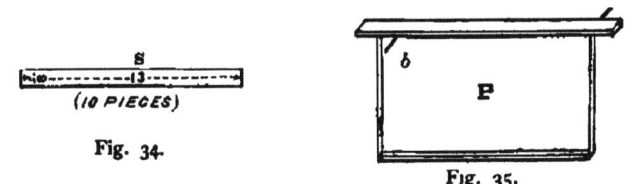

Fig. 34.   Fig. 35.

drive one into the side of the top bar on the left hand side, as at *a*, and one into the opposite side at *b;* these pins are for distance guides, and should project 19-32nds of an inch.   The frames may now be placed in position, resting on the zinc slips, and allowing about $\frac{1}{4}$ of an inch between the end frames and the sides of the hive (which may be regulated by similar pins driven there) will be found to fill up the interior, and the hive is complete.   But, if thought desirable, a stand may be simply and easily made by taking a piece of quartering (T), 3 by 3 ; cut it as in the dotted lines, and four legs will be produced ; 9 inches of the thin ends should be screwed or nailed (sloping side inwards) on the sides of the hive, which will then stand securely.

It is desirable that all the wood should be planed on one side and all the edges ; but, of course, if the amateur is clever enough, he may plane his wood both sides, and dovetail it together ; or he may strengthen the joinery by nailing over all the exterior angles, tin plate or zinc strips, and these may be had almost costless from old Australian meat tins.   I would strongly recommend that the nails used be the French wire-pins.   They may be had of all sizes, are much easier to drive, requiring no bradawl, and hold very fast.   Now for the expense.   If all the materials have to be purchased new, the wood (including legs) and nails will cost as nearly as possible 5s., to which must be added 1s. for the paint.   All the wood may be bought planed on one side, which only enhances its cost a mere trifle.   Should second-hand materials be used, the cost will be, of course, considerably reduced.   The wood should in no case be thinner than I have specified, and the internal measurements should be carefully adhered to.   It will also be advisable to drive the principal nails in at various angles, and clench them where possible, in

Fig. 36.

order that the sun and rain shall not draw the seams apart.

STEWARTON HIVE.—This is a very celebrated hive in common use about Stewarton, in Ayrshire, where, as elsewhere, it has produced most excellent results ; and when better known, will be found worthy of more general employment. In the Apiarian Exhibition at the Crystal Palace, in 1874, a magnificent display of the

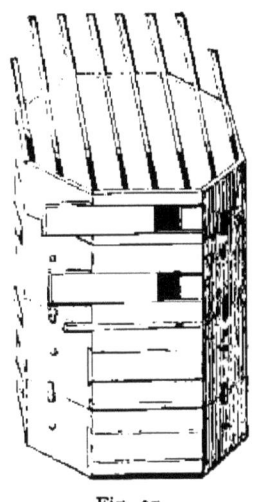

finest white clover honey was made in the Stewarton supers ; the purity, quantity, and beautiful regularity of the combs were worthy of the prize and general high commendation it obtained. This hive is octagonal, with sides strongly dove-tailed together. It consists of two or three body or breeding-boxes, whose inside measure is 14 inches across from side to side, or from back to front. The height of the box, measured inside, is 6 or 7 inches. The bottom is perfectly open. The top is quite flat, and contains usually eight moveable bars or frames, placed

Fig. 37.

parallel to each other in the direction from back to front. The four central bars are framed, and with the bars on either side are $1\frac{1}{8}$ inches wide—the outside bars being $1\frac{1}{2}$ inches wide. The central frames are very useful, affording facilities for examination of the hive whenever desired. The spaces between the bars are capable of being closed by strips of wood, which slide in grooves made in the sides of the bars, and which can readily be drawn out behind when required. Windows with sliding

H

shutters are placed in the back and front of each box, and an entrance is cut out of the front, 5 inches in width by ½ an inch in height. In addition to the set of breeding-boxes, shallow honey-boxes, 4 inches in depth, containing seven bars 1⅓ inches wide, are used as supers. They are furnished with buttons and hooks for the purpose of securing them together, and have no entrance in front.

The accompanying sectional sketch will illustrate the make of the bars or frames.

Fig. 38.   Fig. 39.

' These hives are made in great perfection at Stewarton, and are marvellously cheap. Two breeding-boxes and one honey-box, without floor-board, are, I believe, sold for 12*s.* 6*d.*

An eminent Apiarian, who writes under the *nom de plume* of "A Renfrewshire Bee-Keeper," has written so able an article on the Stewarton hive and system, that I cannot do better than quote it almost verbatim :—

"The general mode of manipulating the Stewarton hive is to lash a couple of breeding-boxes together at the weighing-hooks with cord. After the bars of the boxes have been duly furnished with comb, or embossed wax sheet, run in the sliding door of the upper, and withdraw all the slides of the lower compartments ; then close the openings with the little pegs accompanying the boxes. With the free communication between, the *two* become, to all intents and purposes, *one ;* the Bees may then be introduced—*a prime swarm, of course.* Some eight or ten days thereafter a second prime swarm, if procurable, is hived in the third breeding-box, and at once set down close to the earlier one, and at dusk the last-named is placed on the top of it. The lower of the two first boxes—now the central—has its door run in, and the slides of the lowest are removed and pegged as before. Should the evening prove chilly, a whiff of smoke may be administered to both ; but this is generally considered quite unnecessary, as it is a well-established fact that no Bee leaves with a swarm till it has filled its honey-bag, the lower population now ascends with a most confiding hum, evidently firm believers in the old Scotch proverb, " Plenty freens when ye hae ocht."

" The morning light reveals usually nothing but the surplus Queen dead on the floor-board. The lowest box is then removed, and the entrance of the second again opened. Should any Bees be clustering in the former, the removal can be postponed till the middle of the day, when the Workers will be more abroad.

" The object of removing the third box, is to restrict the room, so that the combined swarms may all the sooner complete comb-building, and packing to the glass, be thankful to press up into the super which has been placed thereon, fitted with guide-comb. Communication between stock and super is afforded by drawing the outer slide only on either side. Should the weather be favourable, and honey abound, it is at once taken to ; if not, it is better to run in the slides again, and wait for a day or two ; then, under more favourable circumstances, make a fresh trial, as it is a curious fact that Bees often will swarm rather than accept a super open to them, which they have previously rejected. Supposing, which is generally the case, the Bees have taken possession, in a very few days white comb appears at the windows ; then, and not till then, the third breeding-box is placed as a nadir underneath all, its slides withdrawn and pegged as at the union, and the doorway of the central box closed once more.

"The colony may now be said to be fairly under weigh, and should favourable honey-gathering weather continue, a second honey-box may be placed on the first, and all the slides of the first super withdrawn. To induce the Bees all the more readily to take to the supers, I have found it a considerable advantage to run a strip of gummed paper round the juncture of the stock with the super, as well as with it and succeeding ones. Should it be taken to, or if honey be plentiful, a second slide on either side of the top box may be withdrawn at first, either partially or wholly. This is a nice operation, dependent on the flow of honey; and the Bee-master must exercise his own discretion, so as, if possible, to prevent the incursions of her majesty into the super. The plan of admitting only the honey-gatherers of the end combs to the supers, to the exclusion of the Queen, the Nurses, and the pollen collectors of the centre, is a most ingenious, original, and, indeed, one of the most valuable features of the Stewarton system. A third and other supers may still be called for, and the additional super accommodation afforded, always uppermost; and, in exceptional cases, even additional breeding space, by nadiring at the bottom, may be requisite, although a strong colony was lately wrought with but eighteen inches breeding space, while filling seven honey-boxes, or supers, in various stages of progress. To get Bees to take to supers at first, and to work in them steadily through the vicissitudes of temperature, it is indispensible that they be well wrapped up with some warm woollen stuff. I generally employ old crumb cloths for this purpose, four plies thick; and need I add that the Stewarton hive being formed of wood but 5-8ths of an

inch thick, it is, of course, requisite, and must have the
protection of a Bee-house or shed from the direct rays
of the sun ; or better still, an outer octagon case, with a
nicely bevelled roof, and an ornamental vase on top, forms
a most picturesque adjunct of the Apiary or garden.

"So soon as the lowest super is seen sealed at the
windows, the attachments between it and the stock and
second super, severed with a thin wire, it had better be
removed, the next lowest taking its place, and so on till
the end of the season. When all are removed, and slides
reintroduced, then, as cold weather sets in, and the
lowest breeding-box vacated, it, too, is better taken
away, the slides replaced, the mouth wrapped carefully
up with paper to exclude moth and dust, and suspended
in any cool dry garret till required the next season."

THE CARR STEWARTON HIVE.—This hive, designed
by Mr. C. W. Smith, is a modification, and, in some
respects, an improvement on the original "Stewarton,"
and is, in my opinion, by far the handsomest hive made,
especially when worked in straw, as shewn in the
woodcut ; it then becomes quite an ornament to the
lawn or garden. It is manufactured by James Lee, of
Bagshot, Berkshire. Combined in it are many of the
advantages of the best bar-frame hives, as well as those
of the far-famed Stewarton. A hive may consist of one,
two, or three stock-boxes and a honey-box. The stock-
boxes are 15 inches square, and 6 inches in depth. The
honey-box is but 4 inches deep. Each stock-box is
furnished with nine moveable wedge-shaped bar-frames,
guides, windows front and back, &c. The honey-box
contains seven wide bars for honey-combs, the spaces
between the bars being fitted with slides, like the octagonal Stewartons. A crown-board, having slats and
slides of the same gauge as those in the honey-box, is

provided, but is reversible, so as to suit the advocates of a close-fitting lid, or those who prefer a $\frac{1}{4}$-inch space above the bar-frames.

Fig. 40.

The stock-boxes can be used separately or together, according to the strength of swarms.

With this hive, stocks and swarms can be united, or artificial swarms made with the greatest ease; and in summer or winter every stock in the Apiary may be properly aided by telescopic expansion or contraction of space, any degree of warmth needful being maintained. It also offers peculiar advantages in the introduction of Queens or Queen-cells to full colonies, as only the combs in one section need be disturbed, whereas in other bar-frame hives, the combs to the full depth of hive must be removed.

There are many other special features in the Carr-Stewarton hive which strongly recommend it for general use. For example, *in Queen-raising*, as each stock-box when placed on a floor-board will form a separate colony of nine frames, and as only four frames will be required for a Queen-raising nucleus, the simple insertion of a close-fitting piece of board in the centre of the box will at once convert it into a pair of nucleus hives, the floor-board being made reversible to form double entrances for that purpose.

At the Alexandra Palace Show, Mr. J. M. Hooker, of Sevenoaks, gained a prize for a hive, "The Alexandra," combining the storifying and collateral principle with the

Fig. 41.

ordinary Woodbury. Fig. 41 shows the general principle

of the hive, as a whole, so well, that but little description is required. The two wings can be cut off from the main body by perforated zinc or diaphragm, or can be used with either frames or sectional supers in conjunction with the breeding compartment. The top, with its two wings, are for sectional supers, any or all of which can be brought into use as required. The hive is glazed all round, which hinged shutters cover. A very fair view can at all times be obtained of the interior.

Hives on the collateral principle seem to have fallen greatly into disuse; although they may still occasionally be found, their advantages are more than counterbalanced by those particular hives I have described.

OBSERVATORY HIVES.—By this term is understood such hives as enable the works of the Bees to be at all times in view. One of the best in use is the well-known NEIGHBOUR'S WOODBURY OBSERVATORY HIVE.—

Fig. 42.

The interior of this hive is divided into six compartments which are formed by as many Woodbury frames run into notches on each perpendicular side; the width of the hive is just sufficient for the thickness of the

combs, allowing the Bees free passage all over ; they
are kept confined by a thick glass door on each side,
which in turn can be covered, and the light shut off by
external Venetian shutters. The framework of the hive
is of mahogany, and the whole revolves on an ingeniously constructed turn-table, giving passage to the Bees
by a tunnel to the external air. It makes a handsome
ornament for a drawing-room or study, placed in a
window ; a small aperture in the window frame will give
passage to the Bees. This observatory hive has the evil
of all other glass hives, the cold nature of its material,
and the narrow width prevents the Bees clustering, the
consequence being that no stock can be trusted to the
rigours of the winter in it ; but its special advantage is
that the framed combs can be taken from an ordinary
Woodbury hive at the approach of summer and returned
to their old place when summer is gone. In such a hive
every Bee can be brought under observation, and when
the Queen be not found on one side turn to the other
and there she must be. This hive is made by Neighbour
& Sons, Regent Street, London.

ABBOTT'S OBSERVATORY HIVE.—This hive, of late

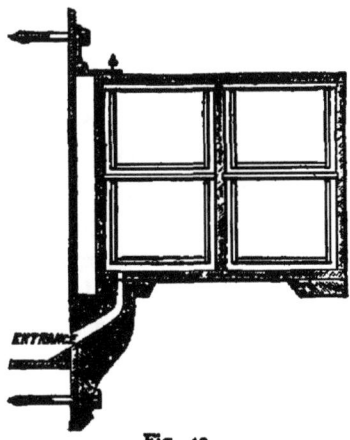

Fig. 43.

introduction, appears to be a very useful form. It is constructed to be hinged on to a door-post, or like position, swinging either way, and when not under observation may be folded back against the post or wall. It is enclosed with glass doors, with or without shutters, and made to hold any number of frames, and an inspection of the figure will clearly show its construction.

Many observatory hives of a more or less fancy description have been designed, and are generally, in their designers' opinion, *perfect;* but other people in practice yet find *much* to be desired.

GUIDE COMBS, AND COMB FOUNDATION.

WHEN using frame hives it becomes an absolute necessity to secure straight combs, and as the Bees have no knowledge of their owner's preference, they are very likely, if untaught, to build their combs the way their fancy teaches them, and they often do not forget that the line of beauty is a curve.

One of the greatest aids to profitable and successful Bee-keeping that has for a long time been devised is that of "Comb Foundation," a name, I believe, of American origin, where the article itself has been brought to great perfection. For many years past, the necessity, when using frame hives, for some guide to induce the Bees to work straight and in the required direction along the bars, has been felt; and in the former editions of this work I described the manufacture of such impressed wax sheets as were then known, but which are

now entirely superseded by the improved manufacture.
A thin strip of old comb, or even a line of melted wax,
put on the top bar of the frame, will be sufficient to
ensure straight building, but this is not all that can be
desired ; for although the straightness of the comb be
secured, the particular construction of the cells is still a
thing to be wished for. Mr. Cheshire made a good step
in this direction by his plan of painting hot wax on a
plaster mould of Worker comb. This the Bees readily
completed; and, with care, Worker cells could be nearly
depended on ; but this plan was troublesome, messy,
and, without considerable practice, difficult ; but now,
since the introduction of the comb foundation, many
important points have been overcome, and we can by its
use, not only ensure that every comb shall be perfectly
straight, but almost that every cell shall be of Worker
size, thus absolutely controlling the birth of inordinate
numbers of Drones, who so severely tax the energies of
their sisters to feed. Comb foundation I will describe as
thin sheets of wax, having its whole surface on both
sides accurately impressed with the foundations of cells,
which may be either of Worker or Drone size, generally
the former for stock hives, the latter for supers. The
cells have shallow walls, which are made sufficiently
thick to provide enough wax for the Bees to draw out
to the full length of the cells. The Bees readily perform this work, and the beautiful regularity of a comb
when so completed is a sight to delight the eye of an
appreciative Bee-master. We must not forget that
comb-building is a great tax on the energies of the Bees,
wearing their lives out fast from the necessary hard
work, and the honey consumed in wax-secreting might
be more profitably employed in filling the cells. At the
present time, every comb in all my hives has been made

from comb foundation, and I have often, 24 hours after supplying the wax sheets, found some of the combs beautifully complete, and already containing eggs and honey. When the honey-extractor is brought into use, the value of these straight combs is very apparent, making the labour of extracting come very easy. The sheets I have used were imported by me from America; many of my friends were supplied from the same consignment, and all, without exception, give it most unqualified approval. The cost of the manufactured sheets in America in large quantities is about 2s. per lb., about one moiety of which is first cost of wax; the latter in England is nearly 2s. per lb., consequently the foundation must of necessity be dearer here. Mr. Root, of Medina, Ohio, who is a large manufacturer of this article, states that in the summer of 1878 his foundation machines were making 1000 lbs. a week, and that four men and a boy could make 400 lbs. per day. This statement will show, that comb foundation need not be a very costly article. My parcels from America, all charges paid, did not come to quite 2s. 6d. per lb. So strong a hold has comb foundation taken on the industry in America, that it is probable the supply of home-grown wax will soon be unequal to the demand. Many experiments have been made with a view of substituting something in place of wax, such as paraffin, and the like, but all have resulted in failure. Paraffin makes a good-looking foundation, but its melting-point is so low that very warm weather causes it to fall. The manufacturers of comb foundation, in order to secure tough sheets that may be used with perfect safety in the extractor, and entirely to prevent stretching, have lately inserted thin wires rolled in the wax sheets. Of course, thus prepared, the combs made on them are not applicable for supers, and their use is yet only an experiment.

The first process, in manufacturing the foundation, is performed by dipping a sheet of galvanized iron in a tall vessel of melted wax, which must neither be too hot nor too cold, and the dipping-plate, which for convenience has a wooden handle, must be kept cold by immersing it in iced water before each sheet is dipped. It is dipped two or three times, until the wax coating is judged to be of the requisite thickness, when the adhering wax is stripped off from both sides. The sheets are now allowed to stand a couple of days to harden, when they are passed between the rollers of the machine,

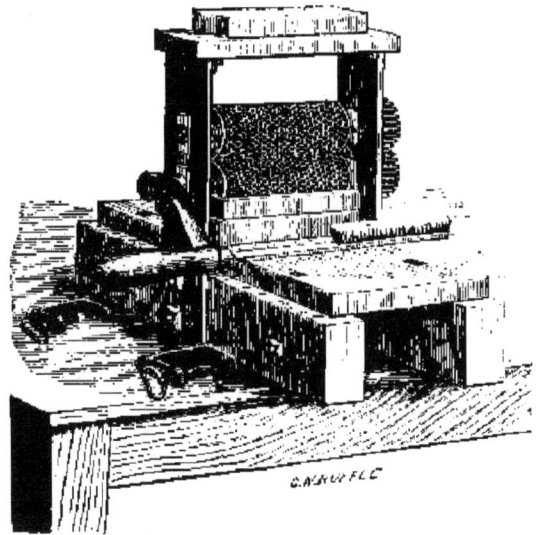

Fig. 44.

requiring only a little trimming to be fit for use. The sheets run from 5 to 8 square feet to the lb., the thicker sheets being by the Bees most quickly made into

combs—and to completely furnish a 10-frame Woodbury hive, requires about 5 square feet, equalling the
consumption of 15 lbs. or 20 lbs. of honey by the Bees.
The comb foundation may be used with equal advantage in starting swarms, as an aid to driven Bees in
autumn, or to replace combs from any cause removed
from hives; for broad combs the sheets should be cut
about an inch smaller in width and length than the
frame, as in process of working they stretch to a certain
extent, and if the frame be completely filled there must
of necessity be some sagging. The way I have fastened
the sheets into my frames, has been by heating some
wax in a glue-pot (as glue), then fitting a board into the
frame not quite half so thick as the top bar is wide, I
lay the sheet of foundation on it, with its upper edge
close along the top bar, then paint the wax along the
joint, and after allowing a few moments to set, turn it
over, and repeat the painting on the other side. Should
the sheet not hang perpendicular, it is necessary to warm
it either by the sun or fire, when it will soon hang plumb,
or otherwise the Bees will attach it to the sides of the
frames, and the comb will not be central.

Mr. Root gives the following as the plan he prefers:—
"If wax is rubbed *hard* against a piece of dry wood, at
ordinary temperatures, it will adhere almost as well as if
put on in a melted state. Therefore, all we have to do to
fasten it in the frames, is to lay it in place, and press the
edge against the comb guide with the fingers, until it
sticks moderately. Now take a knife or screw-driver, and
rub it down hard. To prevent the wax from sticking to
the tool, dip it in either starch or honey; we use the
latter because it is handier. One corner of the tool
should go clear down to the wood, at the last stroke to
make a "sure thing" of it. The foundation should reach

within $\frac{1}{4}$ inch of the end bars, and within $\frac{3}{4}$ as a general rule, of the bottom bar.   This space is needed to allow the sheets to stretch as it is being worked out, which it always does more or less.   Some lots of wax will stretch scarcely perceptibly, while others will to the extent we have mentioned ; and as it is desirable to have the sheet hang clear of the bottom bar when the cells are drawn out full length, we think best to give the amount of space below we have mentioned.

"The reason is, that the combs will bulge if there is any stretching after they have touched the bottom bar.   To put the sheets in rapidly, you will need a board cut so as to just fit inside the frame, and reach up as far as the comb guide.   Lay the sheet on this, close up to the top bar, and stroke it down to the comb guide, as we have directed.   If your frames are made without a comb guide, you can fasten the sheet to the top bar in the same way, and then give it a quarter turn, so that it will hang straight down.   As fast as the frames are filled they should be hung in a hive, to be secure from injury.   If you do not make the above plan work to suit you, you can fasten the sheets by tacking a strip of wood about $\frac{1}{8}$ by $\frac{3}{8}$ into the top bar, while the upper edge of the sheet is between them ; this strip should be put on in such a way that the foundation hangs straight down under the centre of the top bar."

Another way, as given in 'Kings Text Book,' is to lay the frames bottom upwards on a table, placing the wax sheet on the top bar, so that its edge comes nearly across it.   Now take a screw-driver or piece of smooth firm iron, and rub it down hard to the wood until it adheres all along.   One corner of the iron should go clear down to the wood at the finishing stroke.   On this tack a small thin strip of wood into the top bar, so placed that when the sheet is bent up against it, it hangs in the centre of the frame. If the iron rubber be dipped in honey or starch it will not stick to the wax in rubbing.

When a sheet or strip of this impressed wax is properly fixed to the bar, it is certain to be the guide and foundation of a straight comb. It is not necessary, although advantageous, that the sheet should be, when fixed, the whole perpendicular height of the comb; unless we desire a particular sized cell; given a fair start of 3 or 4 inches, the Bees will continue in the same line to the bottom of the frame. For supers, 2 or 3 inches will be found sufficient, and will dispense with the necessity of fixing natural decoy combs. To wax sheets the Scotch Apiarians owe the remarkable and beautiful regularity of their show supers in Stewarton boxes.

SUPERS AND THEIR MANAGEMENT.

SUPERS are receptacles intended to be placed on the top of the hive, for the Bees to store their surplus honey in, and in a great measure to prevent the necessity of swarming.

The quantity and quality of the honey obtained in his supers shows the skill of the Bee-master. Nothing looks cleaner, or could be handsomer as a breakfast-table ornament, than a bright bell-glass, on an appropriate stand, well filled with luscious golden honey. At the Manchester Exhibition of 1873, a glass model of the Crystal Palace appeared filled with 85 pounds of comb and honey; and in 1863, that veteran Bee-master, Mr. George Fox, of Kingsbridge, Devonshire, obtained from two hives glass supers of pure honeycomb, weighing respectively 109½ and 112 pounds net.   As examples of what skilful management can do such results are invaluable, but for commercial purposes large supers are a great mistake.   This was sensibly brought home to my mind at the two Crystal Palace Exhibitions in which I had a large share of the management. Many magnificent supers there shown were all but unsaleable, because of their size.   No private person cared to buy half a hundred weight of honeycomb, and dealers avoided it, for the reason that it could not be retailed economically, in consequence of the waste and mess when cut.   The Americans had discovered this flaw in Bee culture before we did, and seeing this, I immediately took steps to import and introduce to English Bee-keepers examples of sectional supers, which have been readily adopted by advanced Apiarians.   English hive-makers, in manu-facturing sectional supers, have almost invariably over-looked some of the chief advantages of the American patterns, notably their weight and cost.   The former should be so small that the supers may be weighed with the honey, and elicit no comment from the purchaser. Strength and fine workmanship are quite secondary considerations, as they are never intended to be used twice.   At the Bee Shows of 1878 many of these sectional boxes were shown filled with beautifully clean honey-comb, and where ever they appeared found ready pur-chasers at high prices.   So well was this fact demon-strated, that Bee-masters are pretty well agreed that the days of large supers are past, and a new era opened for all those who are ready to move with the times. The enterprizing Yankees so quickly awoke to the fact of England's short-comings in regard to marketable honey, that before four months had elapsed from this

I

Show no less than 80 tons of honey in sectional supers was imported into England! Wake up! English Bee-keepers, and don't buy what you yourselves can produce! As I cannot yet expect all persons to agree with me, before describing these handy little boxes in detail, I must notice one of the best of the larger forms.

For frame hives, square supers—a combination of wood and glass—are very suitable, and are easily made by any handy man, and I give a description of the one which obtained the prize at the Crystal Palace as the best and cheapest super for general use. They are made and sold by James Lee, of Bagshot, at 5s. 6d. per pair; and each holds, when filled, about 18 pounds of honey.

It has very much the appearance of the original Woodbury super, having wooden framework with glass panels; it is 13 inches square and 4 inches deep, and fitted with seven bars. Its construction is a marvel of ingenuity. Made almost entirely by means of a circular saw, every one of its parts is cut to a mathematical nicety, so that they fit each other with great precision, and are all interchangeable with the parts of other supers of the kind. It is composed of two square frames and four ingeniously constructed pillars, each of which is a study in itself; one of the frames is laid upon the table, with the rabbeted side upwards, and a pillar is pressed on to each corner; the glass is then slid into grooves in the pillars, and rabbets in the bottom frame; the top frame is then pressed on to the pillars, and the super is ready to receive the waxed bars, in fact is practically complete, and may be readily taken to pieces. The advantage gained by supers being made to take to pieces is that the honeycomb may be easily cut out for use.

Of course supers may be made of any size, shape, or

material ; the two latter mattering little to the Bees, but much to the commercial value of the honey, whether it is stored in a clean tempting receptacle, or a dirty box. A very strong stock in a favourable season will fill one holding 80 or 100 pounds, and it exhibits the skill of the Bee-master to supply the maximum size that the Bees will fill with sealed comb, as a half-filled super looks very bad.

It is questionable if our Scotch neighbours, who work with the Stewarton hives, are not the wisest: they being content to obtain a number of small full boxes rather than attempt one large one, which will very likely prove a failure as to completeness.

All supers should be supplied with bottom-boards of their own, to be removed with the super ; they need only be made of the thinnest material. Admission from the hive should be given by two narrow slits, corresponding to similar slits in the crown-board ; these are preferable to a central hole, through which the Queen is apt to stray and spoil the contents of the super by breeding therein. Care must be taken to furnish the interior with clean decoy comb or wax sheets, also to well wrap up the super with some warm material, such as felt, flannel, &c., as the Bees will mostly reject a cold unfurnished apartment. Whatever supers (except bell glasses) are used, it is advisable that they be furnished with bars or frames for convenience in removing the honey, otherwise in cutting the combs out much damage and waste are incurred. When using bell-glasses for supers it becomes necessary to furnish the Bees with some kind of ladder by which they can reach the top, for they cannot readily run up the glass sides ; a piece of clean empty comb is best, but many persons use a small clean piece of wood, generally shaped as a cross. Bees are more reluctant to fill glasses than straw or wood supers, and the former require warm wrapping up to ensure success.

When it is desired to use square supers, or bell-glasses, or straw skeps, a wooden platform, as a stand, must be placed on the top of the skep. If the hive is flat-topped it will be sufficient to fasten the wooden stands by means of four long screws through the wood into the hive, but if the hive has a dome top it must first be levelled by means of stiff clay, mortar, or some such material.

To exclude the Queen from supers where she might lay eggs, and so spoil the honey, recourse has been had to the interposition of a sheet of perforated zinc between the super and the hive, the perforations having a diameter of 5-32nds of an inch, permits the passage of the Workers, but not the Queen.

SECTIONAL SUPERS.—These, as I have before said, are the honey receptacles of the future. The little boxes which I had the pleasure of introducing to English Bee-keepers, and for which I had awarded to me the medal of the British Bee-keepers' Association, are those figured in the American periodical, 'Gleanings in Bee-culture,' and made by its editor, Mr. Root; they are used generally fitted into frames either in the upper (or super chamber) or in the main stock hive as end combs. The dimensions of the boxes in question are $4\frac{1}{4} + 4\frac{1}{4} + 2$ inches, and hold, when filled, 1lb. of honeycomb; the frames to contain these sections should be 2 inches broad, and the common frame in America, the Langstroth, holds just 8; these dimensions are not at all material, and the boxes may be made of any useful size to fill the frame.

Sectional supers require to be fitted with a triangular piece of comb foundation, to be presently described; sometimes a saw-cut is made nearly through the centre of the top bar : the wood is bent backwards in such a way as to open the saw-cut : the edge of the sheet is inserted, the cut closed, and all is secure. The foundation may also be fixed in the same manner as described for the frames. It is a debatable point whether the too free use of the wax sheets for honeycomb which is to be eaten is not inadvisable ; some say the comb manufactured on it has a toughness ; others maintain it to be none the worse than comb made from the Bees' natural sources. Experience will teach. The use of these sections with us is yet in its infancy, but in America for several years past ingenuity has been taxed to devise the best form ; some have been manufactured of a very ornamental character, but I think experience is gradually proving that the simplest is the best both for the producers and consumers.

Fig. 45.

Fig. 46.

Fig. 45 shows a complete section box, and Fig. 46 one of the broad frames containing eight of these. These section frames are made the same width as the sections, that is, 2 inches at the top, and 1¾ at the bottom. When in position they occupy the two ends of the hive, the difference in width at the bottom allowing the Bees free passage between them ; they cannot strictly be called "supers," but in this position the Queen will not frequently use them for breeding purposes, if care be taken that she has empty breeding-combs near the centre of the hive. Bees store honey more rapidly in the brood-hive than in the super, but they will seal it more rapidly in the latter.*

For the super, or upper story of the hive, the sections are placed in a case as Fig. 47, which holds three—in the

Fig. 47.

figure, two are in position furnished with guide comb; the third space is empty, to show the position of the tin separator behind. These separators are a sheet of tin, placed between each case of sections, either in the super or brood hive, to prevent the Bees building their combs of varying thicknesses. By this contrivance the whole of the comb is kept within the box, which is, of course, a great desideratum in packing, as they can be laid close together without crushing. The case is made of the same material and in the same way as the sections themselves; it is three times as long, and just high enough for the sections to slip inside, and a sheet of tin 14 inches by 20 inches makes six separators. Both cases and separators may be used again and again, and they serve to keep the sections clean. Propolis may be washed off them when not in use by boiling in weak lye. The ends of the tin are bent at right angles, and sprung on to the case as shown in the figure, or may be dropped into a shallow notch, or lightly bradded on. Thus furnished, these cases are put side by side right into the frames without the interposition of any crown-board. As many should

* A clever manager will so arrange that the Bees shall start and fill the section boxes in the brood chamber, and they may be afterwards removed to the super to seal over—empty boxes, as before, being put in their places.

be put on as will cover the top of the hive and allow the roof to close down ; and when these are nearly full a second story of them may be added underneath the others, raising up the first lot for this purpose.   By this practice the Bees readily commence on the second lot, thus preventing the difficulty often experienced in get‑ting Bees to work in empty supers when their full ones are removed, as by the time the upper tier of boxes are capped over the lower one will probably be half full.   If the Bee-keeper prefers it, any full sections may be removed as they are ready, their places being filled with a fresh box.   The outside sections may be closed with a slip of glass through which the progress of work may be viewed.   The whole should be warmly covered up, for Bees will not fill supers that are cold.   When it is wished to examine the supers, a few puffs of smoke blown on to the top will drive all the Bees below.

The section boxes are sold with the honey, and as they weigh but little over an ounce, are weighed and sold in the same manner as is the paper with sugar.

Fig. 48.

SHIPPING AND RETAILING CASE FOR COMB HONEY.

The filled sections are sent to market (sometimes neatly glazed on all sides) in a crate or case, as Fig. 48.

This contains 48 of the 1lb. sections, and, so far as experience goes, may be sent safely anywhere by ordinary carriers without injury, for the men can see what it is. The crate, if kept clean, and treated to a coat of new paint occasionally, makes a very pretty case for retailing from, for the grocer has his honey neatly cased, and always in plain sight, and when a cake is sold, all he has to do is to raise the cover, and hand it out.

Such sectional supers as I have described are made by machinery, and sold in America any size up to 2 + 5 + 5 for about 25s. per thousand, and should be made for something near the same price here. Until they are so, I would advise Bee-keepers to club together and import such as they require.

Much of the success in obtaining honey in supers depends on the hive on which the supers are placed. It is very difficult to give a date when this should be done, so much depends on the condition of the stock and the weather. It is not well to put the supers on too early, and still worse, too late; the happy moment should be when the Bees have just begun to find more room is required. If they become fully alive to this fact, they are apt to start Queen cells, when the supers will be neglected, unless the Bee-master can wholly excise the royal cells. Should the end of April be warm, and the Bees busy, as a rule we should supply all strong hives with increased accommodation, as often from the late fruit-blossoms we may reap an early harvest. After the fruit and whitethorn blossoms have fallen there is generally an interregnum of a few weeks when supers will not be readily commenced, but in June we may fairly expect to get our main harvest well in progress, and at this time the Bees, both for swarming and honey-gathering, require our greatest attention.

A super should have interposed between it and the

crown-board of the hive a floor-board (or, as it is generally called, an adapting board) of its own to be removed
with it ; it may be severed from the attachments of the
combs by a thin wire or string.   When removed the
super will probably be thickly populated with Bees, who
will be reluctant to leave ; if a Bee-trap be used, their
riddance is easy, but in default of that appliance, some
trouble will be found. If the combs be on bars or frames,
remove them one at a time, and brush the Bees off ; but
if they be fixed as they would be in a glass, remove it,
turn it up, and many Bees will fly home.   It had better
then be covered up for a short time secure from robbers,
again turned up, and more will go ; repeat this until
clear, or if it be taken into a room the Bees will fly to
the window, which may be afterwards opened to give
them exit.   Some instructions on this subject will also
be found under the head of Drone and Bee Traps.

Should any breeding have taken place in the super,
search must be made for the Queen ; if she be found she
must be returned at once to the hive.

THE HONEY-EXTRACTOR OR SLINGER.

THIS is a modern invention borrowed from the
Germans, improved in America, and still further in
England.   The figure illustrates the machine for which
the first prize was awarded to Mr. Cowan at the 1876
Bee Show, and it will give a good idea of the instrument, so that I will merely say that the can is
made of galvanized iron, 20 inches in diameter, by
24 in height, and forms a fixed reservoir, with an outlet
closed by a treacle valve near the bottom, intended
to let out the honey when extracted.   Within the reservoir is a revolving four-sided frame of wire-work,

held in place by a central spindle working in the bottom of the can, and the frame of the top.   The turning of the handle gives motion, which sets the internal wire-frame revolving.   The machine is chiefly applicable to frame hives ; full honeycombs with their frames are taken from the hive, the Bees smartly shaken or brushed off, then if the honey cells are sealed, they are carefully shaved off with a bent knife heated in hot

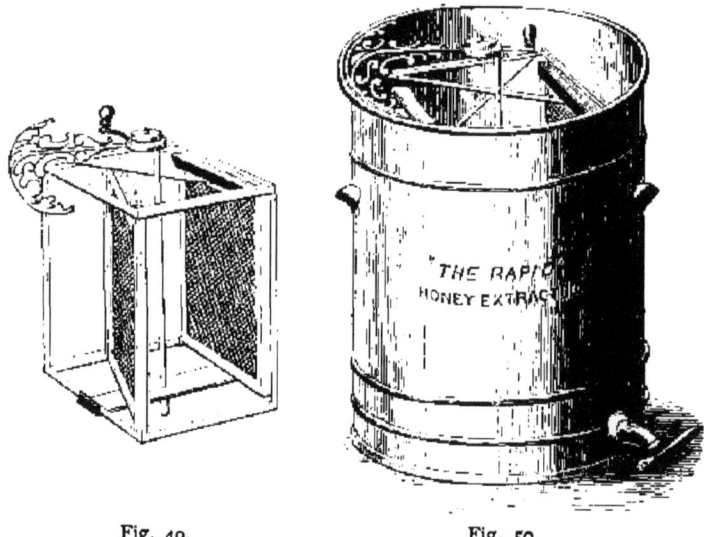

Fig. 49.   Fig. 50.

water.   The frames are placed in the wire cage of the machine ; a few turns of the handle and the honey is by centrifugal force whirled from the outer side of the combs into the can : when one side of the comb is emptied, the wire cages may be reversed without removal, and so bring the second side of the comb to the outside, when a few more turns of the handle will empty that.   Every uncapped cell will now be found drained of its honey, and the frames may be at once returned to the Bees to refill.

The machine requires a little practice before the greatest amount of skill is acquired, after which it will be found to do wonders. Experience soon teaches how to give just that amount of speed which will throw out the honey and not the brood, should any be there, and by a little contrivance, pieces of combs out of frames can be emptied. The acquisition of this appliance is a step in the right direction to get the greatest possible amount of profit from the Bees, at the smallest possible expenditure of Bee labour; and I will now show how the extractor helps us here. In the midst of honey-gathering it is often found that the Bees *will not* work in the super, charm we ever so well; therefore, they hang out idle. We remedy this by taking out a few combs, emptying and returning them, when a general ardour is created to fill them again. In the midst of summer and a good honey season, Bees will sometimes gather so much that every available cell is filled.

The poor Queen cannot find a place to lay her eggs, so suffers in her health, and the contingencies of Bee life being many in the busy season, the stock absolutely dwindles, and perhaps dies subsequently, from nothing else than over prosperity. The danger of such a state of things being discovered, the extractor provides an immediate remedy as in the former case. If the emptied combs are placed in the middle of the brood nest, the Queen immediately fills them with eggs at an astonishing rate. Thus also breeding may be at any time encouraged by empty combs placed in the centre of the hive, as will be further explained. I heard a very practical Bee-keeper remark that he deprived his Bees of *all* their stores, for which he could get 1s. or 1s. 6d. per pound, and returned his labourers for their winter sustenance, sugar syrup, which cost him not more than 3*d*. per pound ; it answered quite as well, and indeed went further.

Our American cousins, from whom we get many valuable Apiarian hints, commonly manage their Bees thus: Two strong stocks are selected which we will call A and B ; from B all the Bees with their Queen are driven, making a strong new swarm ; the hive, with its combs full of brood in all stages, minus its floor-board, is then placed on A, which has previously had its crown-board removed, and an adapter substituted. The Bees of A immediately take possession of B, hatch out all brood, while the Queen remaining in the lower hive still keeps breeding, and the immense population thus formed quickly fill the emptied combs of the upper hive with honey, which, as fast as filled, or nearly so, are emptied by the extractor, and returned ; by this means a very large harvest is obtained, which has amounted to as much as 600 pounds from a single hive. Wax is a product made by the Bees from honey, and it is said that it takes 20 pounds or more of honey to make one pound of wax ; therefore every pound of comb saved for the Bees represents at least 20 pounds more honey to be harvested. Now it is quite a mistake to imagine that old combs, that is to say, up to three or four years old, are useless except to melt down. For breeding purposes they are quite as good as new ; and, indeed, when the Bee-keeper handles his combs much, they are better, being tougher. I would quite as soon have my hives furnished with old combs as new. By the use of the extractor, therefore, we get all the honey and save the combs ; and it will be found where a hive full of clean combs can be given to a swarm, they get a start in life for which they will amply make returns.

When the Bees are busy gathering honey the extractor

may be used in the open air without much trouble, but at other times the operation must be peformed under cover, or at least not very near the hives, or the Bees will soon find out the prize to be recovered and interrupt operations.   The following instructions given by Mr. Root are short and to the purpose.   "The best time is when they are busy in the fields, and if the yield is good, you will hardly need any smoke.   Carefully remove a frame from the hive, and then with a series of sudden jerks shake the Bees in front of the hive or on top of the frames, as you may find most convenient.   When you have shaken off as many as you can, take a bunch of asparagus tops, and gently brush off every Bee in front of the hive.   Now with the honey-knife carefully cut the

Fig. 51.

cappings from all capped cells : to do this quickly you will slide the knife under the caps in such a way as to have them come off in one entire sheet.   When the comb is uncapped it is to be placed in the Extractor; although you can extract one comb at a time if you chose, it is much better to have two, as they then balance each other, and the friction is less on the bearings.   Turn just fast enough (and no faster) to throw out the honey, and there will be no danger of throwing out the brood; you will soon learn this by practice.   Combs so full of brood that there is but little room for honey had better be left in the hive ; there is little to be gained by working very close, and should the honey season suddenly close, there is danger of the Bees starving, as we have known them to do, even in July.

" If your hives are kept close' to the ground, and no weeds allowed to grow around the entrances, there is very little danger of losing Queens while extracting, yet it is a very good plan to keep them carefully in mind, and if you should not see them, we think it a little safer to shake the combs that contain much brood, so that the Bees fall directly into the hive.

" After the honey is taken from one side of the comb it is, of course, to be turned, and the honey taken from the other side. When the combs are very heavy and the honey very thick, it may be best to throw it out only partially the first time, and then reverse, to avoid crushing the combs into the wire cloth by the great centrifugal force resulting from such a weight moving at a rapid speed."

QUEEN CAGES.

BEES, on losing or being deprived of their Queen, will not with any certainty accept a stranger without some precaution ; on the contrary, will often slay her forthwith ; but it is found in practice that if a Queen be confined some twenty-four or more hours amongst the Workers the regicidal tendency abates, and love and reverence succeed to hatred, if the Queen be in a fertile condition. An infertile Queen is not readily accepted, instinct seemingly acquainting the Bees that she is useless. The prudent Bee-master, therefore never introduces a new Ligurian, or other Queen, without tem-

porarily confining her.   In strengthening stocks by the
addition of other Bees, it is also advisable to secure the
reigning Queen for a day or two as a precautionary
measure against the malice of the strangers.   For this
purpose cages of various patterns are used.

The most simple form is that of a coarse wire gauze cup,

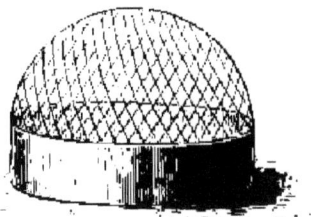

Fig. 52.

with a $\frac{1}{4}$-inch tin margin soldered on, as Fig. 52.   The
Queen, with or without a few of her own Workers, is placed
therein, a card slipped underneath to keep her there, and
then transferred to the comb where it is desired to fix it.
The card being now withdrawn, the cage is gently
pressed down with a screwing motion into the comb as
far as the bottom of the cell, there to remain the necessary time.   It is advisable, if practicable, to tie it there,
as the Bees, in their anxiety to get at the new Queen,
will sometimes undermine and hoist it up, when the
Queen may get out too soon, perhaps meeting an execu-
tioner.   In fixing this cage, select a comb near the
centre of the hive where there is some honey, so that
her majesty may have food at hand.   This is not absolutely essential, and in straw skeps the cage may be fixed
on the bung at the top, care being taken that there is
sufficient space beneath when replaced for the Bees to
crowd about it.

Mr. W. Carr has invented a very simple and perfect
Queen cage which any mere novice can make in a few

minutes. He thus describes it : " It is made of perforated zinc, and measures 1¾ inches long, 1 inch wide,
and 1 inch deep. One side of the
cage has an opening (A) 1 inch long
and 3-8ths of an inch wide, and
this is covered with a flat door (B)
sliding over it on the inside, with
a piece of wire (C) about 12 inches
long fastened to the top of the door
to draw it up ; D is the open side
of the cage to be pressed into the
comb.' The cage is intended to be
lowered down from an opening at
the top of the hive into the centre
of the brood-nest; and after the
Queen has been confined the necessary time, the wire is to be gently
pulled, which will open the door,
allowing the Queen to walk out
without disturbance. The cage
may be removed a day or two
afterwards. Many Bee-keepers dis-
countenance the use of zinc, on the
ground that it is injurious to the
Bees. I question, however, if this
objection be well founded with
ordinary care in cleaning."

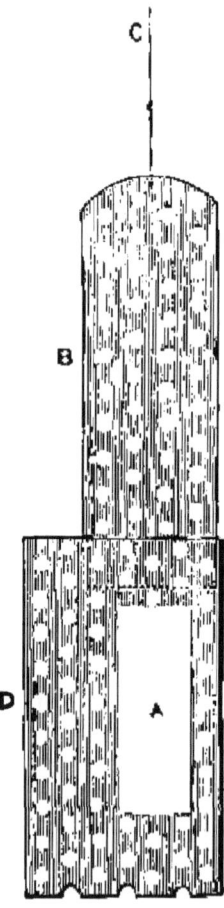

Fig. 53.

The cage invented by the well-
known Apiarian, " A Renfrewshire
Bee-keeper," which obtained the
prize at the Crystal Palace Show, is thus described by
him.

" It is formed from wire net, 2 inches deep by 1¼
wide, and 3-8ths in thickness, the top of the same

material and projecting 1-8th part all round as a flange, to prevent slipping too far between the combs. The door of wire forms the bottom of the cage, and is opened and closed by means of a wire passing up either corner in front, and wrought through the top. In some there is a circular hole on top with movable cover, for introducing the Queen to the cage. But to any, saving the merest nervous novice, the space between the wires at bottom is amply sufficient for the admittance of the royal person. Some are circular for bung-holes in common straw skeps; but I give the

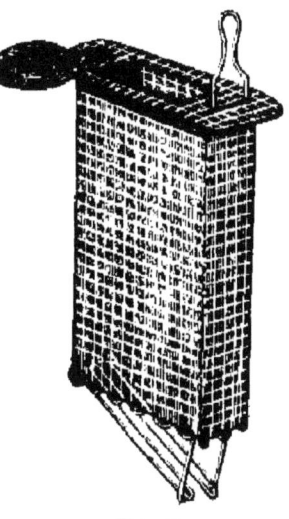

Fig. 54.

preference to those of the flat form, as they fit the exact space between the combs of any hive. Some, for appearance sake, are constructed of copper wire net; and some, to prevent the rusting of the iron wire, are japanned; but they could be made of galvanized wire.

"*Advantages.*—From its thickness it fits the unvarying width of space between the combs of all hives alike. The flange portion on top, resting on the frames or bars, prevents it slipping into the hive. In hives possessing slides it is only necessary to divide a central one, drawing the outer portion sufficiently to receive the cage. The Queen is to be admitted to the cage through the aperture between the central wires at bottom, while the operator holds it inverted, with the door open, in his left hand, the forefinger and thumb of which cuts off her retreat sideways; she is then shut in, and the cage

K

suspended in the hive. On the lapse of the requisite time (third day) the Queen is liberated by simply pressing the top of the wire downwards, which throws the door open, converting it into a gangway, by which she walks forth to meet the attendants who have been feeding her, and are familiar with her presence; they form her body-guard, and the risk of encasement is reduced to the minimum. With all cages stuck into the combs, the Queen can only be set free after the hive has been opened up, and the Workers, being newly and thoroughly disturbed, are in their most irritable mood. Should the pipe cover cage set in a bung-hole be employed, it is requisite to draw it out and invert it, the attendants clinging to the bottom of the cage are transferred to the outside of the hive, and the Queen is forced to stem the upward stream of stranger Bees trying to force their exit. This cage permits the Queen to be liberated without the smallest disturbance to the hive generally."

Bee-keepers are not agreed as to the time necessary to keep Queens confined; some think three days, others are satisfied with one, and I have known six hours sufficient, her majesty walking out in safety after the lapse of that time. In using the wire cage of the Renfrewshire Bee-keeper, it will be perceived that it is not thought necessary to provide the Queen with any food; and I and others have been so sceptical as to doubt that Bees who are anxiously seeking an opportunity to destroy the Queen would yet feed her. That they will do so occasionally is certain, but it is only when honey is freely coming in; at other times they will ruthlessly let her starve, therefore it is safest to cage her majesty on some full honey-cells. Failures in introducing Queens will now and then occur whatever care be used, and they must not always be attributed to the cage. There are many more varieties of Queen cages in use, and, of course, there is no reason why any Bee-keeper should not make modifications to suit his own case or fancy; but the patterns described will illustrate the principal systems in practice. Releasing the Queen in the dark without disturbance has its advantages, but I prefer to watch her majesty's reception by her new subjects, as it is often possible to prevent a regicidal attack, as is described under the head of "Ligurianizing"—there is too much trusting to chance where the door of the prison is simply opened and the prisoner left to her fate; but where the Bee-keeper is at all timid, of course the cage that may be opened from the outside is preferable. The simple cup and Mr. Carr's cages will occasionally be found useful to cover ripe Queen-cells in order that the destruction of the young unhatched Queens may be prevented. When two Queens meet, a duel is most likely to occur. Like two gladiateurs, each first takes a good look at her antagonist, then rush to the fight; they seize each other by legs and mouth, making, with curved abdomen, every effort to insert the sting between the rings of the other's body; they wrestle thus, rolling over and over until one succeeds in giving the deadly stroke. It has been stated that if they get in such a position that both are likely to be stung together, they will separate and commence the fight anew.

> "With mighty souls in narrow bodies prest
> They challenge and encounter, breast to breast,
> So fixed on fame, unknowing how to fly,
> And ultimately bent to win or die;
> That long the dreadful combat they maintain
> 'Till one prevails (for one alone can reign)."—VIRGIL.

It is not, however, from the personal animosity of the

reigning Queen that a stranger has most to dread, but from the vengeance of the Worker Bees, who are more often the assailants and executioners of the intruder.

FEEDERS AND FEEDING.

MUCH ingenuity has been exercised in designing an apparatus for feeding Bees, but they may all give place to a simple bottle, which I think most Bee-keepers of experience use; and, therefore, as the main appliance answering every purpose, I shall describe no other, simply illustrating the best manner to use that. In the first place the bottle selected should be of a squat shape, with a wide mouth; in default of better, pickle-bottles answer admirably. The capacity should be one or two pints; this is filled with syrup, tied over with a double fold of net or leno, and inverted perfectly upright over the feeding-hole, or without the net, covered with a piece of perforated zinc, and then used in the same manner; there being no vent, of course the liquid remains in its reservoir, unless sucked out, which the Bees are not backward in doing; a strong stock will, when active, take in and store one or two quarts in 24 hours, but it is not always desirable to allow them unlimited provender; to control this Mr. F. Cheshire has introduced a simple contrivance by which the supply may be regulated to the Bees, with the greatest nicety. A plate of vulcanite (but tin or zinc will do as well) is fixed upon the hive board by a screw (A), to receive which a hole is first made in the vulcanite with a red-hot wire.

The central circle represents the feed-hole of the crown-board, which should be situated exactly between

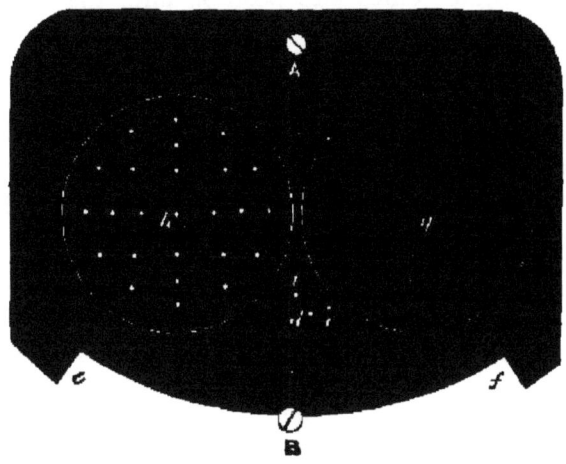

Fig. 55.

A and B; the latter, a locksmith's screw or drawing pin, is placed so that its head laps over the edge of the plate and holds it in position, while it permits its rotation as far as the stops e and f. The plate is pierced, as per pattern in figure, by a heated knitting-needle, the burrs removed by scraping, and the under side roughened by a sharp knife, so that the Bees may have foothold. If the whole has been arranged as described, and the feeding stage turned until the stop f touches the screw B, the circle on the right will be over the aperture in the crown-board, and as this circle contains no holes, the Bees, although the bottle may be on, will get no food; but if the stage be now slowly turned back again, the hole c will pass over the feed-hole, allowing only one Bee to regale herself at a time; a further movement, and d is reachable from beneath, next the hole near the

edges of the left hand circle, allowing two and then
three Bees to sip at our sweets, and as the plate turns,
hole after hole comes into position until the maximum
is reached, when the stop at *e* arrests the revolution of
the vulcanite. For liquid food the bottle and feeding
stage are all that can be desired ; no one at all pretend-
ing to improved Bee-keeping will suffer a hive to exist
in his Apiary without a hole in the crown ; if not origin-
ally there, let it be cut, and a small square of wood fixed
on the top with plaster of Paris will give a level stage

on which to stand the
bottle, of course not
forgetting to cut the
corresponding round
hole in the wood.
With the use of a per-
forated feeding-stage,
such as I have de-
scribed, it is not ne-
cessary to tie over the
mouth of the bottle,
or to use perforated

Fig. 56.

zinc, and as the stage is intended to be a fixture, the following little appliance is used to invert the full bottle
without spilling the syrup : Of zinc, tin or galvanised iron,
is made a small shovel, as in Fig. 56, about 4 inches
square, exactly after the model of an ordinary ash shovel
without the sifting holes. The bottle having been filled,
the shovel (concave side down) is placed on the mouth,
and the whole inverted and stood on the feeding-stage ;
when there, the shovel may be withdrawn, leaving the
syrup at the disposal of the Bees. If it be desired to
remove the bottle again before it is empty, all we have
to do is to slide the shovel under it and invert as

before. If made strong enough, this little instrument will also be found useful as a scraper to clean floor boards, supers, &c.

FEEDING.—Having explained the means by which food may be administered to Bees, I will now say when, and in what quantity, it should be given. At the time a swarm issues, the weather is generally fine; but it sometimes happens a change takes place, and the swarm having no stores, and not being able to gather any, of necessity suffers. Such a contingency happening, the prudent and merciful Bee-keeper will give food at once, not too fast, say half a pint of syrup per diem; if a superfluity be given, the swarm will occasionally construct Drone combs to store it in, which is not desirable. Bees, when they swarm, seem filled with an uncontrollable impulse to build combs; this is a necessity of their future existence, and it is of the utmost importance that the impulse should be fostered and encouraged. The Queen cannot, of course, lay an egg without a cell to put it in, and as she is capable at this time of laying 2000 or 3000 each day, the waste to their owners will be easily seen, should all these embryo Bees be lost. Old stocks in the spring have their stores at the lowest ebb; the winter's consumption has not been made good; and unless the prudent insects find food is coming into the hive, no great amount of breeding will take place. Of course the earlier Bees breed, the sooner they will swarm or store in supers; and in a great measure breeding may be induced at the will of the Bee-master. As soon as the weather will allow in the spring, every stock should be examined, and if found deficient in food, it must be administered. In cold, damp weather, too much syrup is not good; there is no objection to sufficient being given for daily consumption, but the Bees must not have enough given to fill their combs, or the damp arising from it will very likely cause dysentery, and if over supplied they will be apt to store it in the centre combs, being the nearest, and these are all just which should be left for the Queen's use. Barley sugar is a very good food for such times, and may be given to the Bees either in a bottle, or put into the hive, not too much at a time, or it may liquify and form a trouble as well as waste. Barley sugar, superior to that bought at confectioners, may be made as follows, viz. :—

Break up three pounds of loaf sugar, place it in a saucepan or preserving pan, and pour half a pint of cold water upon it and half a wine-glass full of vinegar ; these are all the ingredients required. Prepare a fire in a grate, the top bar of which will let down in a similar way to that in an ordinary kitchen grate, taking care, however, that at the commencement of the operation the bar is up in its place, and the grate full to the top with glowing cinders or wood embers, so that a great heat may be obtained without any flame. The saucepan containing the sugar place upon the fire and stir it without ceasing. In a few minutes it will begin to assume the character of dirty broth, which will have anything but a nice appearance, but presently a thick scum will rise, and the mass will try to boil over. As soon as this is observed, the saucepan should be removed from the fire until the ingredients have cooled a little, when it should be set on the grate again in such a way that only a small part of it is over the fire ; the boiling will then go on on the exposed side ; and, as the ebullition takes place, the scum will be forced to the side not over the fire, whence it may easily be removed with a spoon. Thus the saucepan is held in the left hand, the spoon in

the right, and the saucepan being on the left-hand side
of the grate, with its right side exposed to the action of
the fire, the scum will retreat to the left or cooler side,
and will be in the handiest position for removal, as will
be evident in a few minutes to any one trying it. After
a quarter of an hour of this treatment, the mixture will
have become in a great degree clarified, when it should
be removed from the fire, while the top bar of the grate
is let down so as to permit of its nearer approach to a
greater heat. Should there be any irregularity of the
fire it should now be corrected, but flame should be
prevented, as the mixture having parted with its water
will be liable to take fire if brought into contact with
flame. It will be well here to remark, that so long as
the scum remained on the syrup, there was a tendency
in the whole to boil over, since the water evolved in the ·
form of steam, while the boiling was going on accumu-
lating in a body, would lift the scum above the saucepan
to enable it to escape ; but when the scum was *gone*, the
water would be evolved in bubbles of steam, which
would *crackle*, but not boil over, unless a very intense
heat were applied. The duration of the boiling of the
clarified syrup, before it becomes liquid barley sugar,
will depend upon the amount of heat, and the conse-
quent evolution of the water, to which it is subjected ;
but trials may, from time to time, be made by dropping
a little on some cold surfaces to see if it becomes brittle,
and when that state is arrived at it is done. Pour it into
a tin dish, set it in a dry, cool place until it becomes
hard, and then by striking the tin on its underside, the
whole of the barley sugar will be splintered into fragments, when it may be placed in bottles and corked up
for use as required. As Bees require pollen, or its substitute, *meal*, in addition to saccharine food, it is sometimes

supplied to them incorporated with the sugar. In making the barley sugar as much as one-fourth or one-fifth by weight of flour may be added, and carefully stirred in when boiling.

Those who wish for early swarms and strong stocks will do well to feed slowly in March or in April, even although the stock has plenty of stores; one of Mr. Cheshire's feeding stages will be found an admirable aid to effect this properly. The object aimed at should be to afford a *constant steady supply without a break;* if the stage be used, as much as the Bees can suck through two or three holes will be sufficient, this will be perhaps one-third or one-fourth of a pint daily; so long as this supply be kept up, so long will the Queen lay, and the Bees tend the young; *but* if the supply be stopped for a day or two, and nothing comes in of Nature's providing, the Bees will destroy all the young larvæ, and even those almost ready to emerge, should famine appear imminent. In May and June, when bad weather succeeds a few fine weeks, the Bees may often be seen carrying out their nearly mature young in thousands. When feeding is continued during the day as well as night, take care the supply is well protected against robber Bees, or it will lead to fights and slaughter.

Bee-keepers often express astonishment that their Bees, after wintering all right, die in the spring; the cause is easily explainable : the stock had enough honey to last the winter, but not sufficient to supply the large demand of spring, when the young put in their claims on the commonwealth.

When a stock has become very weak and impoverished, the Bees often display such lassitude that they do not accept the proffered food; in this case they may be excited by pouring into and amongst the cluster half a cupful or more of the syrup made warm: they will then set to work cleaning one another, and gain strength and inclination to make use of the remainder. Bees in straw skeps may also be fed at other times by pouring syrup in a fine stream into the combs; this will run into the cells and be afterwards properly taken care of by the Bees; the quantity given must be regulated by the weather and other circumstances, bearing in mind the caution I have given as to dysentery.

A small swarm, which if left to itself would infallibly die, may be often built up into a moderately strong stock by slow and judicious feeding, such as I have described for spring stimulation. The regularity of a small supply will induce the Bees to build Worker comb, and as fast as built, the Queen will stock it with eggs. If too much food be given it will be a misfortune, the cells being filled with honey where should be brood. Autumn feeding should be on a totally different plan to that I have been writing of—then the one object is to get the Bees to store enough in their hives to last the winter. Towards the end of August every hive should be examined, and such as do not contain at least 20 pounds of honey should be fed until that weight be reached. The weather being warm, the syrup will soon evaporate sufficiently, so the Bees may be supplied as fast as they can take it. A strong stock will have no difficulty in storing away a quart of syrup in 24 hours. If the hive be not fully supplied with combs, this liberality should not be exercised, or too much Drone comb will be made, which is not desirable; better by far first persuade the Bees, by slow feeding, to make the comb, and then give them the wherewith to fill it. It is a common practice to obtain Bees by means of driving, either by gift or purchase, from those who would otherwise destroy them in the autumn for the sake of their stores. These Bees, by slow feeding, may be induced to fill their hives with combs and stores, but the experiment is troublesome and costly, and those who have other stocks would find it better to join the poor castaways to their more fortunate sisters, which will benefit all parties. Such a beaten out stock of Bees would consume 30 to 40 pounds of honey to bring them into a fit state to winter. Syrup, as a Bee food, may be made as follows, and the present low price of loaf sugar, which should alone be used (about 33s. per cwt.), is a great advantage to the Bee-keeper, as this article is undoubtedly the best for general feeding. If a strong syrup be made of it by boiling with water, the sugar will either recrystallize as the syrup cools, or subsequently, as the water evaporates. If it be used in this form it is liable to solidify, or, as the sugar-baker calls it, grain, after it has been deposited in the cells by the Bees; should this happen, they will be unable to feed upon it. This may be effectually prevented by adding to the syrup while boiling a small quantity of vinegar. The amount of vinegar necessary varies with its strength; but about a tablespoonful of that in general use will be sufficient for 4 pounds of sugar, which will make with two pints, or 40 ounces of water, a syrup of the right consistency, and which should boil for 10 minutes after the vinegar is added: 20 ounces of water measure a pint. Rather more water may be used early in the season, when the Bees are breeding rapidly, because they then need a thinner syrup to prepare food for their young than is required for store for winter consumption. After preparing this food put a little of it upon a piece of window-glass, when it should grow stiffer simply without losing its transparency, as the water dries out of it. If crystals are formed, and it becomes white and opaque, it must be reboiled with a little more vinegar. Instead of vinegar, cream of tartar may be used, of which a quarter of an ounce must be added to four pounds of sugar. This food will at the present time cost about 2s. 8d. per 14 pounds, or a little over 2d. per pound.

Honey is, of course, the most natural food to give to Bees, but sugar syrup answers equally well, and is far less valuable ; and, unless the source from which the honey comes is known to be pure, there is a danger of introducing with it " Foul-brood." Foreign honey is said to be very often contaminated by this plague. Those using frame hives, where the frames are interchangeable, will often be able so to arrange their combs as to save much trouble in feeding. Some hives have more honey than they require, therefore can part with a comb or two to their poorer neighbour, and thus the stores may be equalized.

POLLEN.

THERE is another food that Bees, when breeding, cannot do without, that is " Pollen " or " Bee Bread," which, with honey, is masticated by the workers, who form with it a kind of chyle, which is supplied as food of the larvæ. There is seldom any absolute necessity for the Bee-keeper to trouble about providing pollen, the Bees generally having stored, or being able to gather, sufficient. But the Americans and Germans have been in the habit of supplying a substitute for this in meal. Dzierzon, early in the spring, observed his Bees bringing home this substance from a neighbouring mill before they could procure a natural supply of pollen ; and so, not losing the lesson, it became a common practice to supply the

Bees early in the spring with this article. Shallow troughs are set in front of the Apiaries, filled about 2 inches deep with finely ground unbolted rye meal ; and Langstroth says: " Thousands of Bees, when the weather is favourable, resort eagerly to them, and, rolling themselves in the meal, return heavily laden to their hives. In fine, mild weather, they labour at this work with great industry, preferring the meal to the *old* pollen stored in their combs — thus they breed early, and rapidly recruit their numbers. The feeding is continued until the blossoms furnishing a preferable article, they cease to carry off the meal. The average consumption of each colony is about two pounds."

Taking this lesson from our neighbours, many of our English Bee-keepers have during the last few years supplied the Bees with such artificial pollen. Pea-meal appears to be the favourite, which, placed in trays sheltered from rain and wind, is on fine early spring days eagerly carried off by the Bees, and it appears to answer the purpose of natural pollen. In the collection of pollen and of honey, Bees unconsciously perform a most important office as agents in the fertilization of flowers, by transferring the pollen from the stamens to the pistil. Darwin, in his ' Origin of Species,' says that red clover is wholly fertilized by Humble Bees, and as in Australia there are none of the right kind, there they can never raise red clover seed. In many plants the stamens and pistil are situate in separate blossoms, and even on separate plants, and where they are contained in the same flower self-fertilization is often difficult or impossible, sometimes by the relative position of the stamens and pistil, sometimes by their not coming to maturity at the same time. The Bees in seeking for honey and pollen, carry the latter from flower to flower, by this means ensuring fertilization. It is a remarkable fact, that in most cases Bees confine themselves in each journey "to a single species of plant." Thus the grand law of Nature, forbidding the union of relatives, is carried out by Bees, who by their visits from field to field, and flower to flower, give fertility and vigour to vegetable life. A good deal of pollen is carried home by the Bees, adhering to their hairs and bodies, but the chief means of conveyance is the pollen baskets in their hind legs, where it is packed by means of the middle legs. When fully loaded the lumps of pollen are very conspicuous on the Bees as they alight at the hive, within which they quickly run, and arriving at the proper storage place, they stand over the cell, with the legs so placed that on loosening the loads with the middle legs the lump of pollen shall fall into the cell. This happening, the Bee pushes it with its head safely further in, and then sallies forth for more, leaving to the Nurse Bees the job of ramming down the pollen into a compact mass, which they do with their heads. From the various colours of pollens so stored, the successive layers in the cells have a very curious appearance. When the cell is filled it receives a little honey on the top, and then is capped with wax like the honey-cells. Mr. Cheshire records how he mixed some flour in a large tray with a considerable quantity of fine chaff, placing in the corners the trimmings from a comb of honey, the odour of which experience had taught him would soon draw an appreciative crowd. The tray was placed about 10 A.M. in the midst of forty stocks, and on returning in rather more than three hours, he was delighted to find the tray, with its contents, almost hidden from sight by hundreds of earnest Bees engaged in packing the flour into the hollows in the legs, generally called the pollen *baskets*, and strangely enough the pieces of combs, although not nearly emptied of their honey, were receiving no attention. The chaff appeared to answer the purpose of supplying the Bees with a resting-place, much more satisfactorily than bran or any other material yet tried, and it is clear that in the mixture the chaff should considerably preponderate. It was observed that where only a small quantity of flour remained the Bees appeared to work most comfortably. Diving in their heads, and getting a dusting on the under side of the thorax, they just rose upon their wings in order to gather up, and duly stow away the supply, when they made a second plunge, adding what was thus secured to the small pellets already noticeable upon their legs. Another dive or two, and the little rascals, fully loaded, flew away right merrily to their hives. Pea-flour was now supplied, and was commenced upon immediately; but did not, so far as could be traced, attract the Bees more than that first given. The most economical, probably the most useful, plan is, to cover the bottom of the tray with the pollen substitute to the depth of from half an inch to an inch, put sufficient chaff over it to nearly cover it from view, then slightly stir the surface. The chaff will continue to sink as the food is removed, and afford thus during several hours a convenient stage for the little foragers.

Mr. F. Sontag, a German Apiarian, says that he fed one of his colonies with rye-meal placed in a hive in an old comb, continuing the supply till they could obtain fresh pollen abroad. This colony produced four strong swarms that spring, and an adjoining stock not supplied with the meal only one weak swarm.

DRONE AND BEE-TRAPS.

`HESE are sometimes of considerable service in an
\piary, either to capture undesirable Drones or to clear
super of Bees. Of the former kind the Drone trap
1ade by R. Aston, Newport, Salop, has been found very
seful, and is thus described by its maker.

Figure 57 represents it fixed to a Woodbury hive.

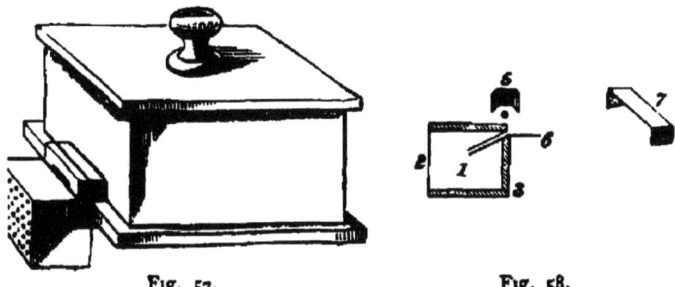

Fig. 57.   Fig. 58.

ut it is only necessary to alter the shape of the zinc
ridge to make it fit the front of a straw skep. The
ap is left on until filled, or as long as is desirable ; it
ffers no hindrance to the Worker Bees, and should the
!ueen stray into it, she would have to stay there until
:leased by her owner. 1 is a sectional view of the Drone
ap ; 2 is a perforated zinc front with apertures 3-16ths
: an inch in diameter, which permits the exit of the
/orker Bees only ; 3 is an opening left at back to place
:fore a Bee-trap when fixed to a super, so as to catch its
'rones ; 4 is a glass tube down which the Drones march
eely into the cage, but cannot find their way back again ;
is a contrivance through which the Workers can pass
: ordinarily, but it has a strip of wood along its centre
hich darkens the way and renders it less attractive
.an it otherwise would be to the Drones ; 7 is the zinc

bridge which may be fitted to hives of a circular shape, yet, when reversed, will be found equally serviceable for plane-fronted hives. The trap is fixed to the hive by the piece of zinc, No. 6, which is screwed to the floor-board, and is held up by a support from the ground or by two light strips of wood which are thrust under the floor-board and catch two nails or pins in its sides.

There are several other Drone-traps in use, but the principle of all is the same, *i. e.* to give the Workers free egress and ingress, but the Drones only the former. Workers can pass through an aperture 3-16ths of an inch in diameter; Drones cannot. ·

What are generally known as *Bee*-traps, in contradistinction to *Drone*-traps, are intended principally for clearing supers of the Bees when taken off the hive.

We will suppose the Bee-master has been successful, and finds on his hive a well-filled super; now comes the

Fig. 59.

operation of removing it, and ridding it of the bees. Many people find this last a formidable job, and sometimes make such a bungle of it that robbers are attracted, to the loss of honey and beauty. My friend Mr. Cheshire suggested a very simple and inexpensive contrivance, which will be found very useful: he styles it the five-pin Bee-trap. On this the Rev. J. L. Zabriskie has made an improvement, which I will now describe. The drawings are from the 'Bee-keepers' Magazine,' of New York.

The first requisite is a box (fig. 59), dark when closed, and large enough to hold the super, or any number of them ; holes three-quarters of an inch in diameter are bored in the front of the box, and the traps, as fig. 59, are hung or tacked over these holes. The trap is made of a block of deal seven-eighths of an inch thick by three-quarters wide and 2½ inches long. Half the block is chamfered or sawn off, as in the drawing, which will give a sloping face to the block when in place. A quarter-inch hole is bored through the middle of the block, and two staples of wire, about the thickness of an ordinary pin, are fastened one above the other below this hole. The staples are inclined upward, and are of such a width that a pin being dropped between from above can easily traverse them, and yet they must be narrow enough to prevent the head of the pin from slipping through, and its body from being pushed sideways much beyond the centre of the hole. A third square staple (fig. 60) is placed close above the upper round staple, and its points driven in until its horizontal part lies tightly against the

Fig. 60.   Fig. 61.

face of the block. The head of the pin rests on this square staple, and the metal surface relieves the slight friction which sometimes might prevent the point of the pin from dropping into its proper place.

When the apparatus is in use the super is placed within the box (of course in such a position that the Bees

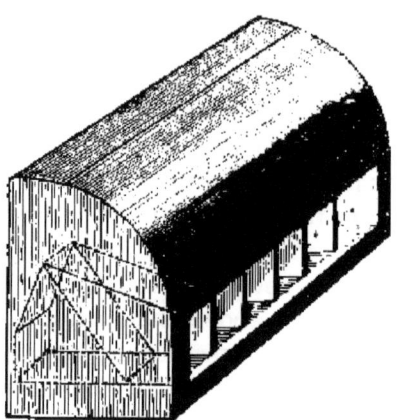

Fig. 62.

can leave it), and the lid closed down.   The imprisoned Bees will soon be attracted to the only light—that which comes through the traps ; here they will easily pass out, one at a time, by pushing the pin outwards, which each time drops, and effectually prevents the entrance of robbers.

Traps are also made on the same principle, having thin plates of talc or horn hung on a wire, and made to fall like the perpendicular pin described above, such as Aston's Bee Trap. (Fig. 62.) In lieu of placing the supers in a box, the super chamber of the hive might be fitted with a Bee Trap (closed by a shutter when not in use), then it would only be necessary to shut off the communication with the hive below, and leave the Bees to make their exit at their leisure.

QUIETING BEES.

" With sprinkled water first the city choke,
And then pursue the citizens with smoke."—VIRGIL.

WHEN performing any operations on Bees, either
depriving them of their stores, making artificial swarms,
or transferring from one hive to another, as well as the
thousand and one things that an experimentalist finds
himself called upon to do, it becomes very desirable to
subdue the Bee's anger, or so to manage that they shall
never become irate ; and many schemes have been pro-
posed for this purpose, but they have nearly all resolved
themselves into one grand solatium "Smoke." Chloroform and burning fungus used to be the means practised,
but it was found that although they recovered from the
insensibility produced, the health of the Bees suffered—
so now "Smoke" has taken their place.

To those persons who are smokers nothing is easier
than to light up a long clay pipe, give a good deep draw,
and while the smoke pours out freely, apply the small
end of the pipe to the hive's entrance ; but with ladies,
and with those to whom the pipe is an abomination (as
it is with me), some other means must be adopted.

The instrument for which Mr. Cheshire obtained a
prize at the Crystal Palace, for its simplicity and utility
(Fig. 63), is formed of a simple briar-root tobacco-pipe,
costing about 6*d.*, which is partly filled with tobacco or
rags. A lighted fusee is dropped into the bowl, over
which a piece of India-rubber tube, one end of which is
plugged up, is placed as shown in the engraving ; then,
by alternately pressing and releasing the tube in the hand,
smoke will be driven out of the small end of the pipe,

and may be directed where desired.   Another instrument was invented by the Hon. and Rev. H. Bligh,

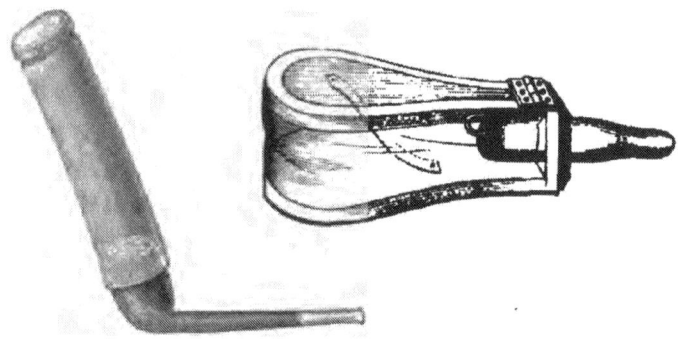

Fig. 63.   Fig. 64.

either as a simple "Quieter," or fumigator to insensibility; for the first purpose, the nozzle is removed and the tobacco placed within it, then being replaced, the working of the bellows will eject the smoke where directed.   For the latter purpose (seldom, in my opinion, desirable) the tube is first fixed into a wooden delivery pipe; the puff-ball torn in small pieces is then crowded into the tube.   A lighted vesuvian thrust into it, the wooden mouth-piece inserted, and the instrument is ready for use.   The simplest smoker of all is a roll of cotton rags, an inch or more in diameter, and rolled just tightly enough to burn and not to blaze.   At times a little tobacco is sprinkled between the rags, and rolled up with them; the great fault in these smokers is their constant inclination to go out, so that ofttimes when most required no smoke comes.   In America they use instruments so contrived that they will keep alight a long time.   There are three of note, known as the "Quinby," "Bingham," and "Novice's" Smokers; they are all good, and answer the purpose well. From 'Gleanings in Bee Culture,' I extract a description of how to make one of the last-mentioned, which, without saying it is *the best*, will, I am sure, be found a very useful instrument.

A soft smooth piece of sheep-skin, 2½ inches wide, and 22 inches long. Also two narrow strips, ¼ inch wide, and the same length as the above. Two boards 5 × 6 inches, and about 5-16ths thick, are all that is necessary to make the bellows.

A strip of wood ½ inch wide, and the same thickness as the boards, is securely bradded to one end of each board, as shown in Fig. 1. These strips are somewhat thinner at one edge, as shown.

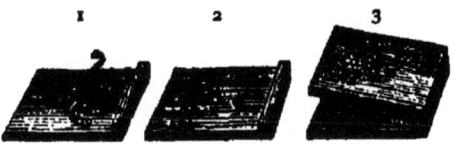

Fig. 65.

Figure 2 shows the upper board, with a single ½ inch hole bored near one end. Fig. 3 shows the two in place, just ready to tack the leather on. The springs shown at Fig 1 are made of bits of clock spring, to be had of any jeweller for a trifle. Bend the springs to the shape shown in the cut, and rivet the end to the wood by two secure rivets. Steel springs sometimes break, it is true, and you can use similar ones made of brass, if you choose ; these never break, but they almost always lose their elasticity sooner or later Those called alarm springs are soft, which makes it easier to work the bellows. Some prefer a stiff spring. Bend the springs so that the boards will come up promptly, as far as the leather will allow. To make a neat job, the leather should be

put on with tinned tacks, about 7-16 in length. Put the
boards as closely together at the end where the hinge is

Fig. 66.

as the two strips will allow them to come, and tack one
end of the long piece of leather. The boards should be
separated at the other ends as far as the width of the
leather will allow. Draw the latter close up to the wood,
and tack at intervals. Now tack the $\frac{1}{4}$-inch strip on for
a binding. When the tacks are all in (they should be
a little more than $\frac{1}{2}$ inch apart), pare off the surplus
leather with a very sharp knife. Finish off everything
neatly with sandpaper, and the bellows is done| which
thus made should not cost more than one shilling, and
be as good as anything in the market, for this price.

As air flows more rapidly through an orifice that is
made smooth with the corners rounded off, the hole in
the upper board should be rounded off on the inside

corners, or, what is better, a short tin tube, with a slight taper and the inside end made flaring, might be inserted ; this may project through the board, $\frac{1}{4}$ or $\frac{3}{8}$ of an inch, when you will find it blow right well, and will probably look something like this :

Fig. 67.

The bellows thus made is merely to supply the air to the smoker proper fixed to its upper surface on the nearly spherical form, as shown overleaf.

It is easy to build a fire in, and little liable to go out. The obtuse nozzle is also easy to clean, and if the fuel be cut small, it may be fed without taking off the cap at all, which is desirable when the case is hot. The tin cup, shown below, is 4 inches in diameter, and $2\frac{1}{2}$ high, and the nozzle is made to shut closely over it. I prefer about a $\frac{1}{2}$-inch hole for the exit of smoke. It remains now to show how to attach the whole to the bellows and damper.

Fig. 4 represents the bottom of the smoker cup. The large hole in the centre is to allow the blast of air to

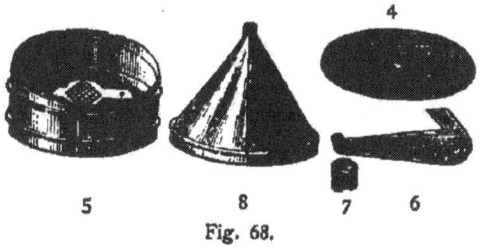

Fig. 68.

come up through, and the smaller ones are for four common screws that attach it to the bellows. To prevent the fire from falling through the large hole, a piece of tin is cut as seen within Fig. 5, and punched full of holes, so as to leave a deep bur on the upper side. This allows the blast to pass through, but no fire ever gets down into the bellows. The holes in the extremities just match those in Fig. 4, so that the same screws hold it securely in place. Now the fire receptacle cannot be screwed directly on to the wood, because the latter would burn; but it has been found by experiment that $\frac{1}{4}$ inch space, between the bottom and the wood, is all that is needed, if the wood is first covered with a sheet of tin. Accordingly, cut another plain piece of tin, exactly like Fig. 4, holes and all; between the two, put short tin tubes, made by rolling up short strips $\frac{1}{4}$ inch wide. These short tubes, shown at Fig. 7, are made so that a screw will just go through them. One thing more, and all is complete. The smoker burns so fiercely, that a damper is required for it. This damper is made of a piece of tin, cut in the shape shown at Fig. 6. When the smoker is put together, the hole in the damper is put just over one of the short tin tubes, and is thus held by one of these same screws. When it closes the central hole in Fig. 4, the end 6 is against one of the other tubes.

It has been suggested that the screws would get hot, and burn the wood, but actual practice shows that the small amount of heat that comes directly on their heads only, never heats them at all. The constant stream of cold air that is coming out and going in, between the wood of the bellows and the tin cup, is probably one reason why it never heats downward so as to affect the bellows. The hole in the centre, Fig. 4, should be sunk by a suitable punch, so as to more perfectly collect the entire blast from the bellows.

The fuel for consumption in this smoker may be rotten wood, rags, corduroy, brown paper, or almost anything that will give off plenty of smoke; perhaps rotten wood is the most economical and preferable fuel. When commencing operations on a stock of Bees, a puff of smoke will be found a wonderful quieter—it should be sent into the hive's entrance or under the crown-board, and the Bees then left alone for a few minutes—the effect is extreme alarm, and in all such cases the Bees rush to their honey-stores, and fill their honey-bags against contingencies. Once filled they are harmless, although of course *all* the Bees do not get into that state. Ofttimes when operating on Bees it will be found advantageous to sprinkle them more or less with syrup; if the weather be cold it should be warmed; this should be poured from a fine rose watering-can; the Bees then become so busy cleaning themselves and their companions that they have no time to think of stinging.

Queen Bees are imported from Italy in little deal boxes about 5 inches square, a Queen accompanied by about a hundred Workers; and on lifting the cover a remarkable proof is afforded of how much our irritable little friends may be subdued. Open the box, there they are, a fluttering, buzzing little swarm, each Bee armed with a sting and two pairs of wings, but showing not the slightest inclination to use either, as harmless as so many flies. Hold the box in hand, they buzz and seem to boil over the edges, running about the hands; and having apparently ascertained all about it, back they go to attend their liege sovereign without any attempt to investigate further, or revenge the indignities they have lately suffered. This state of subjection is the whole secret of driving; it may be summed up in one word, " terror." Only thoroughly alarm the Bees and they become tractable and harmless.

The apathy with which Bees submit to all manner of interference at Bee Shows is mainly attributable to the scare they have received in their journey there—indeed the most vicious stock if tied up and driven in a cart about the country for an hour would be found thoroughly subdued.

When manipulating much with the Bees, the Apiarian soon discovers certain stocks that are much more peaceful than others ; these may be noted as show stocks to one's friends, who will often become quite bold after seeing the way in which the Bees are handled. Half-breeds, the cross between Ligurians and English Bees, have the reputation of being very irritable, and I think it is well founded. When Bees mean mischief, they emit a certain note which I call their angry buzz ; this is soon learned by their owner, who can often avoid being stung by regarding the warning.

FOREIGN BEES, AND THE METHODS OF LIGURIANIZING AN APIARY.

"The better brood, unlike the bastard crew,
Are marked with royal streaks of shining hue."—VIRGIL.

BOTH Aristotle and Virgil wrote of a Bee which answers to the Ligurian, or, as it is sometimes styled, " Italian " or " Alp " Bee, and even in their days it was called the better variety.   The name " Ligurian " appears to have been given by Spinola, who described it in 1805. This Bee has since been introduced into most Bee-keeping countries.   The species is indigenous to the south of Europe, and has been cultivated in Italy in the same way as the common Honey Bee has been in the northern parts of Europe from time immemorial.   It is the *Apis Ligustica* of the naturalist; and though so well known to exist and to have all the honey-producing properties of our own Honey Bee, with some other advantages besides, it seems remarkable that it should have remained so long uncultivated by the Apiarians of this country.   First brought over the Alps in 1843 by M. de Balderstein, the merit of introducing it to this country is due to Mr. A. Neighbour, who, having made the necessary preliminary inquiries, placed himself in communication with Mons. H. C. Hermann, of Tamin-by-Chur, in the Canton of Grison, Switzerland; and on the 19th of July, 1859, the Ligurian Bee was introduced to England.

The Italian Yellow Bee differs from the common Black Bee, in having three light chrome yellow-coloured abdominal bands, each 1-16th of an inch wide.   The Queen is lighter in colour, but otherwise not different in appearance to Black Queens.

The Ligurian Queens are more prolific, their progeny swarm earlier and more frequently, and also work much harder, being abroad both earlier and later.   It has been often said that they work on flowers inaccessible to the common Bee, as their tongues are longer; but, from careful microscopical measurement of a large number, I can contradict this; the size of both Bees and tongues vary, like in the common Bees, but after measuring and averaging many, I found the length practically the same.

Ligurian Bees are now largely cultivated in Britain, and are generally preferred to the common Black Bee; and many Bee-keepers, taking advantage of the fact that the Ligurians and Blacks are both one species (although which is the variety and which the species is unknown to us), and having well proved the theory of Parthenogenesis, have successfully replaced their Black Queens with Ligurians, and so eventually succeeded in Ligurianizing their whole Apiary. This may be accomplished in various ways; the best and simplest is to depose the whole of the reigning sovereigns, and elevate to their vacant thrones fertile Ligurians, which are now imported in considerable numbers at irregular intervals, and are generally bespoken on their arrival; for in the little boxes they arrive in they will not thrive long, and the casualties of the journey are sometimes serious. Supposing these have to be purchased, the expense will depend on the month in which the operation is to be performed. If the Bee-keeper determines to commence his season with the new Queens, they will cost in May or June from 12s. to 15s. each, but if he be content to wait till September, about half the money will suffice.

This is a considerable reduction from their value when first introduced, which was something like two guineas. At the price now obtainable, they will amply repay their speculative purchaser, for there is no question the Ligurian variety is a far better worker and breeder than our old friends. They may be seen sallying forth to work long before the true Britons, and still labour after their neighbours have sought their well-earned rest. The Queens are more prolific, probably because of the above; for whilst food comes into the hive, breeding will go on, and if supplies are stopped, so is egg-laying. The introduction of a Ligurian stock is a general source of benefit to the other Bees of the neighbourhood, for the natural law of " fresh blood " giving vigour holds good with Bees as with larger animals, and very quickly it will be found the progeny of many young Queens will show signs of love-making by the strangers.

The Egyptian Bee has several times been imported into England, but has been found very irritable, with no good qualities to counterbalance this very serious fault. The Carniolian or Hungarian Bee is occasionally imported, and it has the reputation of being very gentle. A stock of this kind I had maintained their good character, but I lost them by disease before a summer's trial was complete. This variety appears to have too great an inclination to swarm to make strong stocks for honey-gathering. On the Continent of Europe great attention has been paid to the introduction of a Bee from Cyprus, said to surpass all others known for good qualities, but very few have been imported into England, and I have no reliable confirmation of their attributed virtues.

The operation of exchanging Queens may be performed in various ways, dependent in great measure on the form of hive in use; with frame hives, ten or twelve minutes should afford ample time for the work, and the danger to the new sovereign is almost nil. With skeps or closed boxes more time is occupied, it being imperative that the Black Queen should be first captured; and, to effect this, it is generally necessary to drive out the Bees until the Queen is discovered and safely removed. Sometimes she will elude the most educated and vigilant eye, in spite of patience and assiduity; and it is unsafe to introduce the new sovereign without being quite certain the old one is not in the hive. The mere fact of not finding her is not sufficient, and in the event of a battle royal it must not be forgotten the foreigner is tired, cowed, and enfeebled by her long journey and confinement, whilst her antagonist is in her accustomed vigour. Supposing the old Queen is surely removed, it would never do to introduce the new one to the tender mercies of the Workers without proper precautions being observed, for Bees are not noted for hospitality to strangers, so she must be inclosed in a wire cage placed in the hive, and kept so imprisoned for at least twenty-four hours, when the excitement of the Bees at the loss of their old Queen will have passed away, and the new one will generally be gladly accepted. It is advisable to sprinkle the Bees and Queen liberally with scented syrup both on the introduction and release. When the above time has elapsed, open the cage gently and let her majesty walk out. Watch carefully the Workers. If they take no notice of her or merely walk over, licking and feeding her, all is well and she may be safely left; but if she be seized by the legs and wings, and the Bees assemble tumultuously about her, beware! In a few minutes the Bees gather into a ball with the Queen in the midst, when regicide is meant. Take up the knot of Bees and drop them into a cup of water, which will effectually separate the cluster and hurt none; or pull off the Bees until the Queen is released, and immediately cage her again for another day's imprisonment, when the same process must be repeated with probably a better result. If a cluster is again formed, try the effect of worrying them about with some tobacco-smoke for a few minutes, when most likely they will give up in disgust.

We must bear in mind that the great secret for the successful introduction of an alien Queen is to familiar-ize the Workers with her before giving them a chance of killing her, for though it is true Bees, in the excitement of driving or swarming, may take a Queen then given and not discover an exchange has been made, and even when they have found themselves to be Queenless and all in consternation gladly accept a new sovereign, the experiment is too dangerous to risk without precaution. It will be at once perceived how, by the proper manage-ment of nucleus hives, enough Queens may be bred from one Ligurian to supply any number of hives, the only difficulty being to obtain pure impregnation; and this where the Drones, either from one's own or neighbour's hives, are English Bees, becomes difficult, and the chances are very much against it. Two or three plans may be adopted to secure this desirable result. Supposing one Ligurian stock is successfully established, Queens in nuclei should be raised; and if the raising of Drones can be prevented in the other hives by cutting out all Drone comb, or the Drones captured as they leave the hive, then supposing the Ligurian stock has plenty of Drones, there is a chance of the Queen's mating with one of those; but it is a poor chance should black Drones abound from neighbour's hives; however, crossed or not, a young Queen should be placed at the head of each stock; and next year (it having been abundantly proved that Drones are hatched from unimpregnated eggs) *all the Drones in the Apiary will be pure Ligurians.* More Queens should then be reared, and (the chance of proper impregnation being now much increased) one should take the place of every Queen who is discovered to have been breeding mongrels. But even a mongrel stock is an improvement on the pure Blacks. Although the first cross Italian is more irascible than the Blacks or pure Italian, it is generally allowed by persons of experience that as Workers they are superior to either pure breed. Bees may be known to be mongrel if they are not all alike. Stocks of pure Ligurians vary in the brilliancy of their yellow bands, but all in the hive will be found to be alike, whilst the Bees of a crossed Queen will be found to vary, some with bright bands, others scarcely to be distinguished from Blacks. Plans have been practised either to breed Drones and young Queens earlier or later in the year than those naturally raised, and success is often attendant. In the first case, a hive should be selected towards the middle

M

or end of March—the two central combs removed and *Drone* comb substituted.   The Queen will fill the cells, and Drones be hatched in due course, by which time young Queens should be ready.   If this be properly managed these Ligurians will be the only Drones about, and on the Queens issuing they may probably be mated successfully; but the danger is the Drones and the Queens not issuing or meeting together ; and if the Queen be not impregnated within three or four weeks of her birth she becomes a Drone-breeder.   Of course if Queens and Drones be bred from selected Queens, in the autumn, after the natural bred Drones are killed, the same result may be obtained.   Drones at this time are best obtained by depriving a hive, when full of Drones, of their Queen, when the former will be suffered to live ; or putting at the head of a stock furnished with Drone comb an unimpregnated Queen who, of course, will breed Drones only.   Mr. Cheshire suggests the following plan to increase the chances of pure impregnation : " The nucleus hive being complete, and its selected Queen cell inserted, place it as near as possible to the stock containing the Drones which is desired to mate with the maturing Queen.   The Apiarian's wishes in the matter will determine his selection.   If the Ligurian be mainly prized for its beautiful markings, the choice will probably fall differently from what it may be if high fertility be chiefly sought.   If the hive admit of it, and one nucleus only is available, it may be placed upon the Drone containing stock, making the openings of the two hives face opposite ways ; the Queen being duly hatched and the time for her flight having arrived, he transfers the nucleus late in the evening to a dark room or cupboard, having previously closed the flight-hole with perforated zinc ; the next afternoon being so far advanced that

Drones are, for the most part, quietly resting from their midday wanderings, the Drone-containing hive is opened and thoroughly warmed, diluted honey is sprinkled over Bees and frames, the cover is replaced, and a food bottle containing the before-mentioned Bee delicacy placed upon it. The nucleus is now brought from its hiding place and positioned as before, care being taken that the sun shines as fully as possible into the flight-hole. Let the nucleus now receive, by lifting carefully the cover, a gentle libation of warm Bee nectar, and shortly, in all probability, the Queen will issue to be joined by one of the Drones, which in large numbers will now be careering in merry mood around the excited stock. Should she fail to come forth, the operation must be repeated on the succeeding day."

A process described in the American Bee Journal advises keeping the young Queen with a few Drones from flying until so late in the afternoon, that all other Drones have ceased flying. The hive or nucleus is then opened, and a teacup full of warm honey or syrup poured a little at a time directly on the cluster. This sets the Bees all in excitement. Very soon the Queen, Drones and all, issue for a flight. If at a proper age (about a week old), the Queen will probaby return impregnated within half an hour. The hive and bees may be placed in a cellar, when the Queen is three days old, and kept there three or four days to prevent chance impregnation.

QUEEN-BREEDING AND NUCLEUS HIVES.

THE practical Bee-keeper will soon see the many advantages acquired by having on hand fertile Queens. Quinby says: "The introduction of a mature fertile Queen to a colony two weeks sooner than when they swarm naturally is an advantage sufficient to pay for extra trouble. The time gained in breeding is equivalent to a swarm." According to Monticelli, the Greeks and Turks of the Ionian Islands knew how to make artificial swarms, and the art of producing Queens at will has been practised by the inhabitants of a little Sicilian Island called Favignana, from very remote antiquity, and he even brings arguments to prove that it was no secret to the Greeks and Romans; but it is not noticed by Aristotle and Pliny. After a stock has swarmed, which takes place usually in the height of the busy time, much time is lost by the parent stock raising a new Queen, and when raised she has to get fertilized, which may not happen for two weeks or more; all this time breeding is suspended, and as mortality is very great in the summer the former strong stock probably dwindles; and if the young Queen on her excursion meets with any mishap, the stock will die, as it then has no eggs or young brood with which to rear another Queen. If the Bee-master be able to supply it with a fertile Queen, immediately on the issue of the swarm, no time is lost—breeding is kept up, and in a few days, if desired, the hive may be induced to swarm again, or the Bees may be set to work to fill a super, provided honey be abundant. By never leaving a hive without a fertile Queen, I may safely say its increase is doubled.

On the Continent of Europe, and in America, there are many establishments devoted to breeding Queens alone, and small swarms for exportation, a large business being done. By these means the Ligurian or Italian Bee has become naturalized in both Continents as well as in Australia, and my object now is to describe how the practical Apiarian can rear any number of Queens he pleases. For this purpose small hives, called *Nucleus Hives*, are used; they may be of any desired size, but it is necessary to work from frame hives of some description. The "Cheshire" Prize Nucleus Hive, which is intended for use with Woodbury hives, is a very excellent pattern; it is $3\frac{3}{4}$ inches wide inside, 9 inches deep, and $7\frac{1}{2}$ inches from front to rear. It has double sides—inner $\frac{1}{8}$-inch wood, outer $\frac{3}{8}$-inch, with strips between, so as to inclose an air-space all round; the back and front have a 3-8th-inch rabbet at the top, similar to a Woodbury hive, for the frames to rest upon. The object of having an air-space all round is, that the necessary heat may be retained, which is very important; and to assist in this it is desirable to varnish or paint the hives white. Mr. Cheshire employs the following ingenious contrivance to facilitate stocking his nuclei. Instead of following the ordinary pattern of Woodbury frames, a little deviation is made, forming what is called "Twin Nucleus Frames." I take the following description and drawings from the columns of 'The Country:'—

Fig. 69.

" A strip of wood, Fig. 69, 3-8ths of an inch thick, and 7-8ths of an inch wide, is cut $16\frac{1}{4}$ inches long, and pencil lines, *b* and *h*, are drawn across it at 5-8ths of an inch from the extremities; the line *e* occupies the centre, exactly 8⅛th inches from each end, and *c, d, e, f* and *g* are placed at 5-8ths of an inch from each other; *k, l, m* and *n* are now added with a gauge-marker, if one is at hand, and *e* being cut through with a fine saw, the parts shaded are removed; the tongue left thus on one half fits into the hollow made in the other, so that the two being shut together, the length of the bar is reduced to 15 inches, and fits the ordinary Woodbury. To the respective halves with brads or small French nails the uprights of the frames, each 8 inches in length,

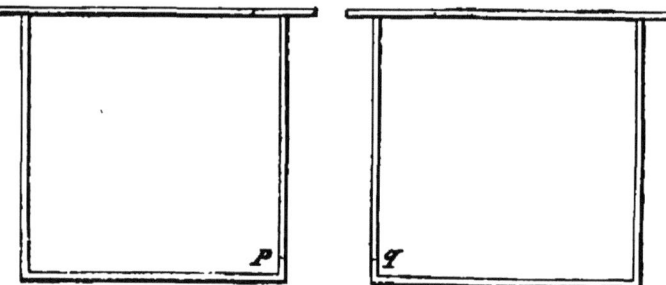

Fig. 70.

are fixed, having their outer faces upon the lines *b, d, f,* and *h;* the bottom bars complete the whole, which takes the form of Fig. 70. If the parts be screwed up in a wood-vice whilst driving the nails, splitting will be effectually prevented. The frames being shut together, holes pierced in *p* and *q,* and a bell-hanger's clip inserted in them, the whole is complete and fit to place in the hive between other frames of comb, or to receive the combs cut from a common frame. The nucleus hives in which the Queens are hatched may be made to take one or two dividing frames. One is preferable for the following reasons: Firstly. A smaller number of Bees will be required to keep up the needed temperature for maturing the Queen at the least 70 degrees in the smaller than the larger hives. They will all be collected on the two combs, and by placing the Queen cell somewhat between, they will be compelled *nolens volens* to nurse it. Secondly. Only half the number of dividing frames will be required in the Apiary that the larger hive would demand. Thirdly. Less combs will be employed; and this, with Bee-keepers who have not many stocks, or who have been fortunate enough to lose none during the winter, is a matter of considerable consequence. Fourthly. Nuclei always dwindle, and only half as many young Bees will be required to strengthen the smaller nucleus hive as the larger would need."

These twin frames, when shut together, form one Woodbury frame, and if, when intending Queen-breeding, two or three of these complete twin frames are inserted into the middle of the hive from which it is desired to breed Queens, the reigning monarch will speedily stock them with eggs; and if she be then removed, her subjects will, after a few hours' delay, convert from four to twelve (or more) of the young larvæ into Queens. Should only a small number of young Queens be desired, and the Queen-cells are sufficiently distributed amongst the twin frames, when they are sealed the frame may be divided, and every such divided frame containing the desired cell removed to a nucleus hive with the cell facing inwards, and another frame of brood placed alongside it. It may happen that some of the small frames have on their combs several Queen-cells; if left there, all but one will be sacrificed, but they may be utilized by cutting them out, and inserting them in other frames not fortunate enough to have Queen-cells of their own. If the parent hive has not been furnished with twin nucleus frames, the combs alone may be divided and fitted into the small frames in the manner which will be found described under the head of " Transferring." It will then be seen that each full-sized Woodbury comb will completely furnish a nucleus hive, wanting only the Bees. It is, undoubtedly, an advantage that each comb in the nucleus should contain plenty of brood, because, as they hatch out, fewer Bees will be required to carry on the work of the miniature colony ; and if it be found that the Bees dwindle too fast, and the brood has hatched out, change one of the empty combs for a fuller one, or place any quantity of young Bees, who have not flown, on the floor-board in front of the nucleus, they will run in and fraternize at once.

Young Bees may be always told by their lighter colour, having a greyish look about them. When breeding Queens, it is not safe to leave a number of sealed cells together more than nine days after the first cell was formed, as, should an older larva than usual have been selected by the Bees for a Queen, it may hatch sooner than expected, when the remaining immature Queens will be sacrificed. When the young Queen hatches, let her remain with the nucleus until she becomes fertile, when she may be made use of either to replace another Queen, or to build up a new stock. The nucleus should be stocked with young Bees, if possible, as they are not likely to go back again to the hive of their birth, and will live longer. A goodly number should be given in order that the two combs may be well covered ; to accomplish the stocking, search for combs having plenty of young Bees on them, then shake them in front of the nucleus hive, taking care to spread a paper or cloth from the entrance to the ground in such a manner as to

prevent the Bees taking shelter *underneath* the hive;
this may be accomplished by slightly raising the hive
from its floor-board, and putting the edge of the cloth
beneath it. The Bees will then run in, and probably
remain; but if next day it be found many have deserted,
repeat the process until a sufficient population is
procured.

The Bee-keeper who keeps himself familiar with the
internal economy of his hives will often find numbers of
Queen-cells in swarming time; the first Queen who
hatches generally destroys the rest, but if Queens are
wanted, the cells as sealed over may be transferred to
nuclei, or to other hives, where a Queen is required.
Care should be taken not to bruise the cell, as the contained pupa is very delicate, and it must not be allowed
to become chilled; so the more quickly all operations
can be completed the better. The cell should be cut
out with a triangular piece of comb attached, and inserted, mouth downwards, in a similar aperture in the
selected comb. Before removing Queen cells, it is as
well to wait until they are nearly mature, which may be
known by the cell having the wax removed from it by
the Bees, so as to give it a brown appearance.

When Queen-cells are sealed over, and the young
Queens due within a day or two, they may be readily
artificially hatched anywhere in a temperature of 90° to
100°. In America a hot water chamber is used by
Queen-breeders for this purpose, and I have even
hatched them in my trousers'-pocket, but unless the
atmosphere be moist as well as warm, the Queens are
apt to have crippled wings, when they are useless. A
curious thing about these artificially hatched Queens is,
that provided they have not been with other Bees, they
may be safely introduced to any colony wanting a

Queen, who seem to pay them no attention whatever. If, however, they have been with other Bees it is almost impossible by any known means to get them accepted by strangers, so long as they remain infertile.

'King's Bee-Keepers' Text Book' describes the following method of procedure pursued in America to form nuclei:—

"Form a nucleus from an Italian or other populous stock, by blowing a few whiffs of smoke into the entrance, and, opening the hive, select a frame of comb containing capped brood, but especially plenty of eggs and young larvæ. After looking this over carefully, lest the old Queen be removed, place it, with its adhering Bees, in the empty hive, and next to it another comb containing honey, which will afford protection to the brood and food for the Bees, as many of the old Bees will return to the parent stock; give the nucleus hive at least a quart of Bees, and set it on a new stand, two or three rods distant. Contract the entrance so that but one or two Bees can pass at the same time, a feeder or sponge filled with sweetened water, set on the frames, will supply their wants until the young Bees go to work in their new location. In place of the combs removed from the parent stock, set in empty frames with a full one between. If the frames are put near the centre the old will increase all the faster, as the Queen will fill the new comb with eggs as fast as it is built. The removal of the two frames stimulates the Bees to great activity by giving them room to work, and detaches just Bees enough to prevent their clustering idly about the entrance. The nucleus will construct Queen-cells, and rear a Queen as well as whole swarms. Besides, the Queen is easily found among so few Bees. We now wait until the tenth or eleventh day from the time the nucleus was formed, when we open it, and with a sharp thin-bladed pocket-knife, cut out all the Queen cells *but one*, and use them immediately in forming other nuclei, by attaching one of them to a frame of comb and Bees taken from an old stock as before described, and placed in an empty hive. The beginner should remove but one at a time, returning the frame from which it was taken to its place in the hive, until the royal cell is adjusted in its new location. When practicable, leave about an inch square of comb attached to the cell, and upon taking the comb or brood from the old stock make an opening among the eggs and larvæ, where the Bees will be sure to cluster upon it, and keep it warm. If the first nucleus was formed from the only Italian stock in the yard, and more Queen-cells are wanted, remove every Queen-cell from it, and add another comb of eggs, and brood from its parent stock. But when no more Queen-cells are needed, leave one to hatch, and as by this time the brood will all be capped over, the Bees will be liable to follow the young Queen on her excursion to meet the Drones. To prevent this, exchange one of the combs for one containing eggs and young larvæ, when forming the other nuclei. Young Queens will return, unless lost, destroyed by birds or other casualties, to which all Queens are once exposed. Such loss is easily ascertained among so few Bees, and we have only to insert another Queen-cell, adding a comb containing eggs and brood, and repeat the trial."

DRIVING

Is the art of compelling Bees to leave one hive for another, either to facilitate the making of artificial swarms, to enable us to deprive the Bees of their stores, to strengthen the population of stocks by adding two or more together, to capture the Queen for the purpose of introducing a Ligurian, or making other exchange. Driving is principally done upon stocks in skeps; with frame hives it is not usually required. The *modus operandi* is very simple, and, properly managed, should seldom fail. Some writers have gone so far as to assert it is simply absurd to imagine that a stock of Bees will leave their well-furnished hive for an empty one at the bidding of the Bee-master. I can only say *they will*, and the stronger and more active the stock, the sooner they will go. On a cold day, with very weak or Queenless colonies, I have sometimes found the Bees unpersuadable, or only going after a long exercise of patience ; but at other times from ten minutes to half an hour is generally sufficient.

At the Bee Show of the British Bee-keepers' Association, 1878, prizes were offered to the competitors who should in the quickest, neatest, and most effectual manner, drive out the Bees from a full straw hive, and capture and exhibit the Queen. The first prizeman accomplished his task in $5\frac{3}{4}$ minutes, capturing the Queen in her exit; another competitor did his work in $5\frac{1}{2}$ minutes, but missed the Queen as she travelled. It has often struck me as surprising how any one can fail to drive the Bees under favourable circumstances ; that beginners do often fail is incontestible, but having once passed the *pons asinorum*,

the successful Bee-keeper feels astonished how he could
have failed in such an easy operation. When once the
work is begun never give in until completed satisfactorily. It becomes only a question of time, *the Bees
must go.* Supposing now it is desired to expel the
whole of the Bees from their hive, and it is the operator's
first attempt to drive, I would suggest the following
method of procedure, which, if followed, will result successfully :—In the middle of a fine day, when a good
many Bees are abroad, commence by blowing two or
three puffs of smoke into the hive you desire to drive,
then give it a smart open-handed smack on each side,
and leave it ; the smoke and the smacks immediately
put the Bees into intense excitement, and after, perhaps,
an alarmed sally to the entrance to take stock of the
enemy, every Bee proceeds to fill herself with honey to
be prepared against contingencies. Whilst this is going
on, get ready a pail or stand on which to set the hive—a
pail is best if the hive is round-topped, as it will be
held more secure ; also two empty skeps, two sticks
about 1 inch in diameter, and two iron skewers, and if
the operator be timid a round towel as well as 2 or 3
yards of stout string ; five minutes will have by this
time elapsed. Now the hive must be boldly lifted off its
floor-board and placed mouth upwards in the pail or on
the stand, and another skep of the same size placed
(mouth to mouth) on the top of it. On the stand where it
came from, place an empty skep to amuse the Bees who
come home whilst we are operating. The round towel
may now be wound round the juncture of the two hives
and secured with the string ; this, after the experience of
a few drivings, will be dispensed with. Now, with the
two sticks, or with the open hands, smartly strike the
sides of the full hive, keeping up a continual drumming ;

the Bees become terror-stricken, and, after a time, start in a stream for the upper hive, giving out a rushing sound which may be plainly heard if listened for. The emigrants are now harmless, and will neither fly away nor sting, consequently the towel may be removed, and the top hive tilted up to an angle of 45 degrees, being kept in position there by the two skewers, with which pin the hives together right and left of their point of junction, which must be at the place where the swarm of Bees is thickest.

Notwithstanding the skewers, the top hive is often found to slip and re-precipitate the Bees on to the combs, and to obviate this, and free one hand, I have designed some little appliances, as Figs. 71 and 72,

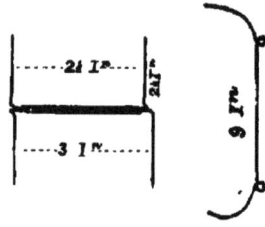

Fig 71.   Fig. 72.

which are made of wire about one-eighth of an inch in diameter, all ends sharp-pointed. The two larger portions of Fig. 71 are united by a coiled wire of half their thickness, the whole forming a complete hinge, the lower pair of points to be driven into the edge of the full skep their full length : the other pair into that of the empty hive, which may then be inclined at any desired angle, and supported in front by the other wire or a pair of them, Figure 72, whose points may be fixed in the straw where needed. After again separating the two hives, if the hinge be left on the one containing the Bees for a time, it will be found useful as a prop to tilt up the hive on the floor-board while the straggling Bees are coming home to their new quarters.

The progress of the exodus being watched, and a sharp look-out kept, the passage of the Queen will probably be seen (unless she has already gone up), when she may be captured, if desired, or allowed to proceed with her subjects; when the stream of Bees begins to slacken look down amongst the combs and, probably, various clusters of Bees will be observed ; start them with a puff of smoke or stir them with a feather, when they will most likely run to join the main body. Experience will soon give such confidence that it will not be thought necessary to tie the two hives together with the cloth, but proceed at once with the open driving, especially if the object be to capture the Queen only, for she is just as likely to go up with the first rush as to stay till the last. Having succeeded in the driving without seeing the Queen, great care must be taken that she be not left behind in the hive, which should be carefully searched. The Bees that have gathered in the temporary hive on the floor-board may now be shaken into the other ; or if it be intended to place the driven Bees on their old stand, they may be left to fly home after being removed elsewhere. If driving is attempted in wet or cold weather, or late in the evening, the Bees will often be troublesome to move; and, as a very little cold benumbs them, numbers who have flown will be lost, from their inability to reach their home, so that this practice should not be pursued at such times without adequate cause ; but should necessity arise, and it be found or thought the Bees will be reluctant to leave, they may be induced to go, by warming their new domicile and sprinkling them with warm syrup, thus creating the excitement necessary. Mr. Pettigrew employs a method of shaking Bees out of a straw skep in lieu of driving, which he thus describes: " When hives are less than thirty pounds in weight we shake them out in less than half a minute ; no smoke is used, the Bees are taken unawares; the hive to receive

them is placed on its crown, the other gently raised off
its board (it must be previously loosened), but not turned
up; the Bee-master now places his fingers inside the
hive and his thumbs outside, the hive being fairly
balanced on his hands, and his legs pretty well astride
the empty hive. He now acts as if he were going to dash
the one he holds against the other, but they never touch;
the Bees, however, go forward, and fall into the empty
hive. A few violent thrusts or shakes, well performed,
is often enough to empty the hive of every Bee. In cold
weather, when Bees are sitting fast among their combs,
they cannot be shaken out without first feeding them
by sprinkling. A few minutes after having been fed
they will be found moving lightly about over their
combs, when they may be readily and easily shaken
out in less than half a minute. We often perform
this operation by candle-light. By feeding the Bees
about sunset, and taking them into a room or barn in
about half an hour afterwards, they can be readily
shaken out on to the floor of the room, and a hive placed
over them, and sometimes there is not a Bee lost by
doing it." This plan may be practised on old hives
crossed by the abominable sticks; but from any others
I fancy the combs would fall as well as the Bees, which
would not be the desirable thing.

TRANSFERRING COMBS AND BEES TO FRAME-HIVES.

A BEE-KEEPER would often use a frame hive, were it
not for the fact that his Bees are at present domiciled in
a skep, and he knows not how to remove them; and as

this is one of the most important operations, requiring some exercise of skill and knowledge, I will endeavour to explain the method to be pursued.

For my own part, knowing the value of the comb foundation, I should never transfer old or crooked combs unless it be for the purpose of saving the brood from destruction. The frames being supplied with the wax sheets, and food given, which may be either syrup or honey, the Bees will soon build out their cells, but if no such foundation be at hand, the old combs may be utilized so long as they are clean and wholesome. Frame hives and the honey-extractor will give every facility for this, and it will be found true economy to furnish all frames with combs whenever possible, and a straw skep full of combs, whose late inhabitants have died or deserted, will furnish for a swarm such a start as will send them far ahead of all competitors not so fortunate. In making use of old combs we are enabled to keep under the production of superfluous Drones, for, if Worker comb be given, Workers will be bred ; and when we wish for Drones, all we have to do is to supply the Queen with Drone cells.

No old comb should at any time be used which has about it the slightest suspicion of foul-brood—better far melt it down or burn it than introduce this malady into the Apiary. All the whitest of the combs, particularly if of Drone construction, should be reserved for furnishing supers with decoys, without which the Bees are often reluctant to work there. For breeding purposes, the colour of the comb is of little import, it will last good four or five years. Strips for guide-combs are best made of the old and tough combs, and are as readily accepted by the Bees. The value of one pound of wax is about 2s. 6d., that of twenty pounds of honey,

N

20s. ; therefore, by melting down one pound of clean Worker combs, the Bee-master loses 17s. 6d. ! Why should not this lesson be borne in mind ?

A novice will find considerable difficulty in transferring the combs of a hive that are full of brood, as the young larvæ are extremely delicate and susceptible to cold, and, therefore, it is by far the easiest plan to allow the stock to swarm either naturally or artificially, and the brood to hatch out, which will all be accomplished to the last egg in twenty-one days after swarming, excepting, perhaps, a few drones ; at this time (a day or two, more or less, will not matter) the combs will be empty and light and much easier to handle. Now let *all* the Bees be driven from their old home into an empty skep, which place on the old spot ; then carry the denuded hive into a room or other place inaccessible to the Bees. An old skep is seldom of much value, and in this case with a strong knife cut it right in half between the two centre combs. The object we have in view is to fill the frames of the new hive as far as we can with the combs from the skep, and in the absence of apparatus, which I will presently describe, lay the first frame down flat on a clean table, and having cut out one of the centre combs, if it be larger than the frame (as is usually the case with centre combs), merely cut the lower side straight, and reduce the height of the comb so as to fit the frame by cutting off as much of the honey-cells at the top as may be requisite, and the same at the two ends, so that the comb shall fill the frame completely, and consist of all or nearly all Worker cells. If there be any portions of the fitted comb *prominently* thicker than the centre part, slice it off with the knife, endeavouring to arrange so that the foundations of the cells shall be equi-distant from both sides. If the comb was sufficiently large, it should now be found firmly fitted to the frame, and can be at once placed in the new hive as far as possible in the same order as the comb was when fixed in the skep, but it is generally advisable to pass a couple of tapes over frame and comb to prevent the latter afterwards falling out of place.   Some of the combs will now be found not large enough to fill the frames; if they be plentiful, cut them into rectangular pieces, and so fill the frame.   The Bees will join all together, and they will soon make a good sound comb; but when combs are scarce, and we cannot afford to waste any, cut the top straight, and if the bottom bar be not reached, support the comb with a wooden lath under its bottom edge, under which pass two or more tapes, tying over the top bar against which the comb should thus be tightly pressed.   If the vacancy between the lath and bottom bar be not much, the lath may be wedged up tightly by means of two or three old corks or like means.   Should the combs not reach along the whole length of the top bar, it is as well to fasten on a strip of Worker comb as a guide for the Bees to continue, or they will probably build crooked.

Care should be taken to preserve as much Worker comb as possible, to pare the thick honey-cells away until they are of the proper thickness, and to put the combs in the right way upwards, that is, as they were built.   Very little Drone comb should be returned, and that placed towards the sides of the hive.   All the parings of the combs, waste honey, &c., should be carefully collected into a feeding bottle, and given to the Bees on the top of the hive ; they will re-store the honey, so that little or no waste will occur, and it will assist them in eliminating wax wherewith to fix and make good the combs, which in the summer will generally be found done in 48 hours; after which, the supports may be removed, being careful in replacing the frames not to damage the fragile new attachments.

Now to return to the fitting. As fast as the frames are fitted, replace them in the hive, and when all are placed, about which no time should be lost, return the Bees as if they were a new swarm — see "Natural Swarming."

If there be not enough combs to fill all the frames, guide-combs should be attached to those empty to insure straight building; and in swarming-time all spare combs should be utilized in this manner.

An apparatus which greatly facilitates this operation

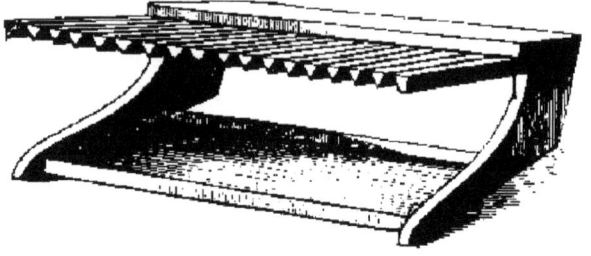

Fig. 73.

was exhibited by Mr. F. Cheshire at the Crystal Palace Show, which he calls a "Transferring-Board." The judges thought its utility worthy of a special prize. It may thus be described: The board consists of sixteen wooden tongues about 10 inches long, fixed like the teeth of a comb; it has legs which, for packing, fold underneath, and a zinc pan to catch the dripping honey. Flat on the tongues is placed the comb to be transferred, and the frame is fitted on to it; a lath is then laid on its edge under the comb, and tapes passed between the tongues, and fastened at once on the top bar. The lath is not required if the frame be quite filled.   The board can then be tilted up until perpendicular, carrying the comb and frame with it, which latter is to be at once lifted out and placed where required.   I have several times used this appliance, and have found it very handy.

DISEASES AND ENEMIES OF BEES.

BEES have not many diseases to trouble them, but the few they have are ofttimes very fatal ; indeed one, which is known under the name of foul-brood, has been justly termed the Bee Plague ; this fatal complaint is far more common than is generally supposed, and to it many a Bee-keeper who has found his Apiary unproductive for years, with stocks dwindling in spite of all care, may with truth attribute his ill-success.   Much has been written and said on foul-brood, but up to the present time it is not thoroughly understood, nor effective means known either for its prevention or cure.   It is not of modern origin, for Aristotle described it more than two thousand years ago.   I may briefly say that foul-brood is the name given to a disease which causes the larvæ of the Bees to die and putrify in their cells, where they turn to a disgusting foul-smelling, semi-liquid mass, impossible for the Workers to remove, in which condition the air of the hive becomes necessarily impure, poisoning the unfortunate inhabitants.

The cause of foul-brood has been much debated, many observers being of opinion that the disease is simply the rotting of brood which had become chilled ; but the opinion seems to be gaining ground that, like typhus and scarlet fever in our human hive, it is solely produced from germs of a fungus, millions of which are floating in the atmosphere, and which, when finding an appropriate habitat, germinate and produce the disease: probably the foulness of dead larvæ provides this condition, and the fungi spores there find the essential condition, as in like manner typhus finds it in squalor and dirt.

Dr. Schönfeld of Germany has made a variety of experiments, which tend to prove the correctness of this theory.

As an example of the destructive effects of this disease, I may cite the case of Dzierzon, the great German Bee-master, who in 1848 had this plague break out in his Apiary with such virulence that he lost more than 500 stocks, only ten having escaped the malady. About 1865, a friend of mine, who had twenty stocks, complained of them not being profitable, and I purchased the whole of him, and removed them to my garden. Alas! they were foul-broody, and I lost them all, and my original stocks in addition, as well as having two or three years of trouble and vexation.

Again in 1876-7 my Bees were attacked with the same disease in a most virulent form; and once more, in spite of endless trouble, and far more attention than most people could devote to their Apiary, I lost them all. Many times I cut out the plague spots from the combs, sometimes destroying all the brood combs. For a time all appeared to go well, but most surely the evil day came again. While the warm weather lasted the combs were examined almost daily; a single foul cell scarcely escaped attention; but when the quiet of winter arrived, the disease spread apace, and in the end I made a clean sweep, by destroying the frames and the whole of my beautiful straight combs that I was so proud of. The hives I had scalded inside and out, washed with a solution of salicylic acid, also with carbolic acid, and then painted ; but even then the "snake was only scotched," not killed, for in one hive, being short of new frames, I used two or three of the old ones previously boiled, and in this hive the disease again appeared, which was immediately stamped out by destruction.   A much-vaunted cure for foul brood is salicylic acid ; several eminent Bee-masters have spoken very favourably of it as having been by them successfully used.   I give the recipe, but in my own case it was utterly useless; although I used it lavishly in the most thorough manner, I was unable to find the least good result.   Herr Hilbert reports that he cured 25 badly infected stocks by the following process : Dissolve 50 grammes (not quite $1\frac{3}{4}$ ounces) of salicylic acid in 14 ounces of spirit of wine, which will be found sufficient for 12 stocks; 100 drops of this solution should be added to one pint of soft water lukewarm, with which the combs and hive should be well sprinkled, having first thoroughly shaken the mixture.   The combs are to be replaced in their hives as soon as the operation is completed, and if no un-necessary delay is made the brood will not be injured. A little of the Salicylic Acid solution is also given to their bees ir all food supplied.   I do not in the least doubt Her Hilbert's veracity, but I think it possible the qurantine after the treatment had not been long enough to determine whether the reputed cure was fallacious or not.   In my own case I several times congratulated myself on a cure, only, as after events proved, to be disappointed.   Where an Apiary is found infected, I am confident the wisest course is to destroy combs, frames, hives, and honey, as well as all tools and litter about the place that has been in contact with the stocks.   The destruction as advised should be by burning, for if any piece of the comb, &c., is left about, and be visited by a Bee, she carries home, perhaps, the germ of further trouble. The Bees may be saved thus: Let them be driven, or by other means taken out of the hive and confined in a straw skep with plenty of ventilation for two days; the act of driving will have induced every Bee to fill herself with honey from her old home; this, if allowed to be deposited in a new hive, would probably communicate the disease to the new combs, but by keeping the Bees confined for the time mentioned, all the honey will be consumed, and the risk of infection considerably lessened. After the quarantine has expired, transfer the Bees again to a clean hive; if they carried infection away from home they will probably leave it in the temporary hive, which, to be on the safe side, should be also destroyed.

Honey that is found in an infected hive should on no account be given to other Bees, and as it comes from an atmosphere of putridity, is not fit for human consumption; so is much better consigned to the flames with the combs, &c. Foul-brood is often introduced into a hive by feeding the Bees on foreign honey which is not seldom infected with it.

One cause of the dwindling of a foul-broody stock is the constant reduction of the number of breeding cells, for when a larva dies it is simply left to rot in its cell, which, of course, becomes useless, and the number of these cells may be so increased that the poor Queen cannot find wholesome ones sufficient for her eggs.

I now proceed to say how the presence of foul brood may be known. If the Apiary has been long unproductive, the Bees showing no energy or increase in their numbers, but, on the contrary, dwindling, *suspect foul-brood;* if extensively present, the combs will give out a bad odour like stinking animal matter, as indeed it is, and on examining the combs they will be found here and there black on the surface, with the cells having their caps somewhat concave, with minute perforations; on removal of the caps the cells will be found to contain a foul-smelling, sticky, semi-liquid, coffee-coloured mass, which may be drawn out into threads like heated glue; the dead larvæ may also be found in all lesser stages of decomposition.   Other cells will be found in which the liquid has dried, leaving at the bottom a mass containing highly infectious fungus spores, from which it may easily be imagined how every comb, Bee, and drop of honey in a foul-brood hive becomes a centre of infection, spreading the disease far and near.   If we at any time discover in the combs dead and rotting larvæ, excise the whole comb, or at any rate such portions as contain the foul cells.   If the disease has not made much progress, it may perhaps be thus stopped, but the combs should receive a thorough examination frequently, to see if any more work for the knife appear.   Dr. Schonberg says, that the disease in its wet state is not contagious, although this is denied by some eminent Apiarians. In manipulating or examining frames containing larvæ, care should be taken that the larvæ do not get chilled and die, for thus may be created just the nidus necessary for the fungus to flourish.

DYSENTERY.—This is another disease, which is some-times very destructive to Bees, and in some phases runs very close to foul-brood, many Bee-keepers yet main-taining they are one and the same thing. Dysentery is a disease of the Bees, sometimes extending to the larvæ. Foul-brood never extends to the Bees.   There is no doubt, however, how dysentery is often caused; improper or too liquid food, cold, damp, and confinement will all

produce the malady.   Bees, it is well-known, are cleanly
animals, and they will not, except under the most urgent
circumstances, void their excrement within the hive.   On
the sudden appearance of a warm, sunny day, after
perhaps a long series of inclement ones, how eagerly do
the Bees fly abroad, and relieve whilst in the air their
distended bowels! Conspicuous places round about their
homes may be seen in all directions, spotted with their
rejectamenta.   When quietly clustering during the winter
months Bees require to relieve themselves but seldom;
but if they are by unnatural disturbance roused into a
state of excitement, with their accustomed impetuosity
they distend their honey-bags by rifling their stores, and
if unfavourable weather succeed, and they cannot fly out,
dysentery is very likely engendered.   The same effect
may be produced by a cold damp hive, whether caused
by atmospheric moisture from without, or by the im-
prudent stowage of a large quantity of watery food,
perhaps given to them in mistaken kindness by their
would-be benefactors.   If a hive be discovered in
this unfortunate condition, with still living inmates, the
remedy is to remove all dead, give dry floor-board, and,
if a frame hive, transfer all Bees and combs to a clean,
dry hive.   Should there be a large quantity of unsealed
food it had better be removed by the extractor or otherwise, and the Bees, if necessary, fed with small quantities
of honey or barley sugar; then, if the population be not
too much reduced, we may hope to save the remainder.

Deaths from chilled brood and starvation cannot be
attributed to disease, but rather accident; and I need
scarcely say if mortality should be found to occur from
either of these causes, the dead should be immediately
removed lest disease should be engendered.

ENEMIES.—In England the enemies of Bees are but

few, if we leave out of the question their inhuman masters of the fire and brimstone school.   Wax moths, although very destructive in America, make no headway in England; that is to say, in hives containing living Bees, although where empty combs are carelessly stowed away they will, probably, be wholly destroyed.   There are two species of moths which commit these depredations; one, the largest, *Galleria Mellonella*, is comparatively rare here, although commonly imported in the larva state with Ligurian Bees; the other, *Achroia Grisella*, is very common, and where combs are left about unprotected, its larvæ will most likely soon be too apparent.   The Apiarian who pays proper attention to his stocks will not need to fear the wax moths.   The death's-head hawk moth (*Acherontia Atropos*) is commonly cited as a robber of Bee-hives, but in England it is sufficiently rare to be unnoticeable in our Apiaries.   On the Continent of Europe a small insect, known as the Bee-louse, *Braula Cœca*, often infects the Bees to a considerable extent, as many as a hundred being sometimes found on a single Bee, and as the insect is nearly as large as a small flea, the poor Bee, when thus loaded, must find her life a burthen, as each louse lives by sucking the Bee; the young are said to be produced in the pupa state.   I have found this pest several times on imported Ligurians; but the climate of England does not, fortunately, appear to suit them, for they have soon disappeared.

Wasps often become very troublesome; they do not hesitate to enter any hive to which they can gain admission.   A strong stock can generally defend their entrance successfully, but woe betide the unfortunate weak colony; there the wasps run riot at their will, and will often completely rifle the hive of all its honied sweets.   These marauders should be trapped in narrow-necked bottles of sweetened beer, which they will eagerly enter and get drowned therein; the Bees are seldom thus caught. Every wasp nest in the neighbourhood should be sought for and destroyed; and in the spring, when only the Queens are in existence, it must be remembered that every wasp then caught prevents the establishment of a nest.

Insectivorous birds are sometimes very troublesome, foremost of which stand the blue tit (*Parus Cæruleus*) and the great tit (*Parus Major*). These birds, in the winter time, when other insects are scarce, find an abundant supply from the Bee-hives. It is said they will stand at the doorway of the hives, stamp, and await the unlucky Bee who seeks to know the business of the visitor; certain it is, that I have seen a rail, a few feet in front of my hives, studded with Bee-stings in hundreds, torn from the unfortunate victims, whose plump and welcome bodies have formed the dinner of the tits, who apparently reject the small portion which might prove to them a discomfort. The fronts of the hives may be fenced with a piece of wire-netting to outwit these unwelcome visitors.

Mice, sometimes, will take up their winter quarters within a hive, feasting on the stores as occasion arises. When perceived they should be captured and destroyed.

> "The titmouse and the 'pecker's' hungry brood,
> And progne, with her bosom stained in blood.
> These rob the trading citizens, and bear
> The trembling captives thro' the liquid air."—VIRGIL.

VENTILATION OF HIVES.

ANIMALS, from the smallest insect to lordly man, cannot live without air; and our little friend, the Bee, forms no exception to this rule. In the midst of summer, when the hive is populated to repletion, the heat becomes intense, and did not the Bees adopt some measures of prevention, the new and delicate combs would collapse and fall, as well as the health of the helpless larvæ suffer. Nature, therefore, has taught the Bees a remedy. If on a hot summer day the entrance of a hive be examined, a number of Bees will be there observed standing on the board with their wings in rapid vibratory motion, which carries in a strong current of fresh air, replacing the hot foul air driven out, and the number of "ventilators" is increased or diminished as occasion requires. By this means the atmosphere within is kept pure and wholesome, as was demonstrated by poor blind Huber. We are thus taught that Bees cannot bear close confinement which, if accidentally occurring, as it does sometimes by the snow or dead Bees blocking up the entrance, will, unless quickly obviated, cause dysentery and death. Apiarians who use hives with movable tops can, in the summer, in great measure, regulate ventilation by leaving the top more or less open by means of a small piece of perforated zinc placed over the feed-hole. If rightly managed, this aid will set at liberty great numbers of Bees, who would otherwise be ventilating, to assist in the general work of the hive, and will often prevent the external clustering to which they are driven by the extreme heat, in order that the combs may not melt, or the young be stifled. The entrance of the hive, if properly constructed, should be capable of enlargement at need, and the Bee-master can, by this means, greatly assist in good ventilation by making the opening larger in summer and smaller in winter. The interference of the Bee-keeper in the matter of summer ventilation I do not consider of much moment; he can certainly assist his Bees, but if that assistance be not rendered, no great misfortune will necessarily follow. It is in winter that defective ventilation is frequently the cause of great calamity—no less than the death of the whole colony; and although I strongly advocate frame hives, I feel compelled to say this misfortune happens more frequently in those domiciles than in straw skeps; but this is no fault of the frames or their construction, but simply that the wood with which they are usually built retains the generated moisture, whilst the straw allows the greater part to filter through. This defect being admitted, I now show how it can be remedied; *en passant* I may say that frame hives can be and are made equally well in straw as in wood, when that objection to them, of course, is done away with; but when we use wood, which is the more common and handy material, care must then be taken that proper ventilation is provided. Much has been written on this subject, but I think the evil has been greatly magnified. When the Bees are thickly clustered together for the winter they do not hybernate like many other animals, but are all lively and require food, in the consumption of which moisture is evolved in the form of vapour—this, if it cannot escape, naturally condenses into water, keeping the hive cold and damp, and the temperature low, obliging the Bees to eat yet more to keep up the necessary heat, and thus the evil is increased.

Upon a due appreciation of this subject, much of the

success of Bee-keepers depends. If we consider Bees as we should human beings, we should not err greatly in the treatment and construction of their domiciles. With proper ventilation, Langstroth says: "No amount of cold that we ever have will injure Bees;" and as he records the temperature of January, 1857, at 30 degrees below zero, which is never reached in England, I do not think we need fear. We all know a cold dry winter is more healthy than a mild wet one, even though the temperature of the latter should be many degrees higher; and a large airy bed-room, with window open, is preferable to a small close one with sand-bags and appliances to keep the cold out. Langstroth cites a case where twenty hives were in a row, one suspended 20 inches from the ground, without a bottom board, the others in the usual condition for wintering. The whole got very wet; the nineteen died, and the one survived, having been able to get rid of the moisture. One of our most successful Apiarians mentioned to me that a hive which gave him a super of 76 pounds weight, in 1874, was wintered without a crown-board, but covered with an empty super, and, as the result showed, with advantage to the Bees.

On making an examination of my stocks early in February, 1875, I found one hive, a part of whose movable crown-board had slipped aside, exposing several square inches of the top freely to the air, but, fortunately, not to the rain. This stock was then by far the strongest of many, and had a fair show of larvæ growing up to Bee-hood.

A wooden crown-board tightly fastened to the hive's top keeps the cold out *and the wet in*, and some means must be adopted to obviate this. When the hive is a simple box, with the combs built from the top, a loose pad should be laid on the feed-hole. The American custom of entirely dispensing with crown-board, and substituting in lieu thereof what is called "a quilt," is very generally practised in England. The quilt is composed of a piece of carpet, or piece of duck, and then a thin mattress stuffed with chaff, or other material, on the top of that; in fact, anything that will warmly cover and yet permit ventilation. Unless the hives be located in a damp place I don't look upon a quilt as an absolute necessity. With my own hives I prefer to let the crown-board remain, and my stocks do not suffer from damp.

PROPOLIS.

> "And with their stores of gather'd glue contrive
> To stop the vents and crannies of their hive,
> Not birdlime, or Idean pitch, produce
> A more tenacious mass of clammy juice."—VIRGIL.

THIS is a resinous substance which the Bees obtain from many trees, and it is applied by them to a variety of useful purposes. It is, I believe, the only one of their stores, if we except Bee-bread, that man has not found it useful to deprive them of. With propolis the Bees fill up every undesirable crevice about their hive, fix the latter to the floor-board, and, often to the annoyance of the users of bar-frame hives, cement the movable (?) crown-board so tightly to the top that it becomes a fixture, and occasions considerable trouble to loosen it. Everything in the hive that is not tightly fixed will soon be put into that condition with propolis. But these are not the only uses to which Bees put propolis. Should dead insects, or other offensive matter, make its unwelcome appearance within the hive, which the Bees are unable to remove, they have a remedy in propolis, with which they will encase the objectionable substance. They will also with propolis firmly cement to the floor the shells of intruding snails, effectually stopping their slimy wanderings over the combs. Reason and Instinct! Who shall presume to say where the line is drawn?

HONEY AND ITS SOURCES.

HONEY is the most important product of the Bees' industry, and the main article for which Bees are cultivated. It may be shortly described as a sweet vegetable juice, secreted in the nectaries of flowers, from whence it is gathered by the Bees. Its chemical constituents are nearly the same as glucose or grape-sugar. Popularly, Bees are supposed to "*make*" honey: they do not do so; they simply gather and store it, after which much of the water it contains is evaporated, until, before sealing over in the cells, it becomes considerably thicker than when gathered. If the Bees be supplied with sugar syrup they will store it, and to the eye it has much the appearance of natural honey; but it is syrup still, as may be proved by tasting. A Bee gathers honey with its tongue, a beautiful flexible instrument, having about 112 joints. It is covered with hairs, and measures as nearly as possible one-eighth of an inch in length. This, inserted into the liquid nectar, is alternately extended and contracted, by which means the honey is passed upwards into the mouth, and thence through the gullet into the honey-bag or first stomach; which is the vehicle for conveyance home; from there it is regurgitated

o

into the cells, where it is left to evaporate. The colour and flavour of honey varies much, according to the floral source from which it is derived. From the white clover and hawthorn it is beautifully white; from Lucerne, golden yellow; from heather, light brown, aromatic, and slightly bitter; from sycamore, very dark and thick; from ivy and laurels, it is often so strongly flavoured with prussic acid as to be disagreeable, and instances in foreign countries have occurred, of honey being actually poisonous, from the plants it was gathered from. As a general rule, however, honey is both delicious and wholesome. As an article of diet it is held in high esteem, and is not unknown in medicine—it enters into the composition of several preparations recognized by the Medical Council of Great Britain, and is a nice and popular remedy for sore throat, cough, &c. Dr. Munro, in his 'Medical and Pharmaceutical Chemistry,' states that Dr. John Hume, one of the Commissioners of the sick and hurt of the Royal Navy, was for many years violently afflicted with asthma. Having taken many medicines without receiving relief, he at last resolved to try the effect of honey. Having had a great opinion of its virtues as an expectorant, for two or three years he ate some ounces of it daily, and got entirely free of his asthma, likewise of a gravelly complaint he had long been troubled with. He also mentions another case, where a very bad case of asthma was cured by the same remedy.

With the exception of an occasional gathering from honey-dew (to be presently explained), Bees gather the whole of their honey from flowers, and, consequently, where there are no flowers they cannot thrive; but the term flowers must be taken in a broader sense than meaning such as we cultivate for garden ornaments or home decoration. The inconspicuous blossoms of many trees, the wee modest wild flower, scarcely noticed by passers by, furnish abundant pasturage for Bees. Many persons who have lived in the country all their lives are scarcely aware that our noblest forest trees have flowers at all, but from the brave old oak and the wide-spreading beech, Bees gather many a pound of honey. An avenue of limes or sycamores, a field of beans or white clover, forms a very El-dorado for the busy Bees, their pleasant hum on the snowy hawthorn, or the sweet smelling sallow (palm as it is commonly called), is very noticeable when Nature is awakening from the gloomy sleep of winter, and our thoughts and feelings are glad with the prospect of returning summer. Where large heaths abound, the Bees have a second harvest, and it is a common practice in such localities for Bee-keepers to send their hives to the moors for about two months, the trouble and cost being amply repaid by the immense weight of honey brought home, which the common heather yields freely during August and September. Mignonette, borage, honeysuckle, hyacinth, crocus, laurustinus, lavender, lily, primrose, and many other flowers are visited by Bees. The arable fields supply buckwheat, beans, mustard, clover, and Lucerne, which all give an abundant supply of honey. Borage has the reputation of being the best of all Bee flowers. It blossoms continually from June till November, and is frequented by Bees, even in moist weather. The honey from it is of superior quality, and an acre would support a large number of stocks. In America much of the great harvest of honey is obtained from the limes and wild sage ; the Bee-keepers are also in the habit of sowing the seeds of many well-known honey-yielding plants on purpose for the use of the Bees.

Dwellers in the country cannot fail to have observed

occasionally that the leaves of the trees and shrubs have a gummy appearance, and are sticky to the touch. If a leaf so covered be put to the tongue it will taste sweet ; this is honey-dew, and is a secretion of some species of aphides ejected from their abdomen in little squirting streams. This substance the Bees readily gather, and when it is abundant, make large additions to their stores.

In Scotland, and on the Continent, cart-loads of hives may be seen travelling to and from the heather. Often on the spot they are looked after by some resident cottager, who receives a gratuity of about 1s. per hive from the proprietors of the stocks. In the south of England this practice is not pursued, although I do not see why it should not be in many places, there being miles of heather equally available as in Scotland. On the Nile there are Bee-barges which travel only at night, stopping in the daytime at any place that affords abundant pasturage for the Bees ; and we read in *Pliny* that this was likewise the practice in Italy in his time. "As soon," says he, "as the spring food for Bees has failed in the valleys near our towns, the hives of Bees are put into boats and carried up against the stream of the river in the night, in search of better pasture ; the Bees go out in the morning in quest of provisions, and return regularly to their hives in the boats with the stores they have collected ; this method is continued till the sinking of the boats to a certain depth in the water shows that the hives are sufficiently full, and they are then carried back to their former homes, where their honey is taken out of them." And this is still the practice of the Italians who live near the banks of the Po, the river which Pliny instanced particularly in the above-quoted passage.

It was the advice of Celsus that after the vernal pastures were consumed, the Bees should be transported to places abounding with autumnal flowers, as was done by conveying the Bees from Achosia to Attica, from Eubœa, and the Cyclad Islands to Scyros, and also in Sicily, where they were brought to Hybla from other parts of the Island.

In the summer of 1878 a revival of this ancient practice was attempted in America by Mr. C. O. Perrine, who fitted up a travelling barge on the Mississippi with 800 stocks. He intended to travel 2000 miles, following the flower-bloom up the river ; but from accidents to his machinery, and the utter inexperience of such a scheme, his trip was a partial failure, not sufficient, however, to deter him from contemplating a future trial another year.

> "Thou cheerful Bee ! come, freely come,
>   And travel round my woodbine bower ;
> Delight me with thy wand'ring hum,
>   And rouse me from my musing hour.
> Oh ! try no more those tedious fields,
>   My honied treasures all are thine ;
> Come taste the sweets my garden yields,
>   The bud, the blossom, all are thine." —SMYTH.

STINGS.

THE fear of being stung deters many people from keeping Bees who otherwise would gladly avail themselves of such an instructive and profitable occupation, and to some persons the fear is well-founded ; for, although the hardened Bee-keeper may treat with contempt the alarm as puerile, the sting of a Bee will often produce a painful and distressing temporary effect. As a satisfaction to those who, in spite of the dreaded little weapons, intend to become practical Bee-masters, I may give them the satisfaction of knowing that they will soon get inured, and mind stinging not at all. Many persons imagine on seeing a man handling Bees with impunity that he is never stung. This is an error ; the Bees do sting him, although not so often as they would a timid stranger; but his blood is inoculated, and the poison has become innoxious. My son, when a lad of sixteen, had not meddled with Bees ; then, becoming often my assistant, he soon had to pay the usual penalty, which was at first very severe. Great swelling and inflammation, accompanied with pain, and often an irritating rash would appear all over his body. The effect of every successive sting became less and less, until before the autumn closed, beyond a few minutes' irritation, there was no effect. Mr. G. Walker, of Wimbledon, has recorded an experiment he made on himself to try how long, and how many stings, it would require to get inoculated. He gives the following as the *modus operandi* and result, viz. :—

" I went to one of my hives, caught a Bee, placed it on my wrist, and allowed it to sting me, taking care that I received the largest amount of poison by preventing it from going away at once; then I let the poison-bag work, which it does for some time after being separated from the Bee. The first day I only stung myself twice. A Bee-sting has always had a very bad and injurious effect on me, inasmuch as it has always caused a great amount of swelling and of pain ; in fact, once when stung on my ear, the part became so painful and swollen that I hardly got any sleep the following night, and it was three days before I recovered. The first few stings I got during this experiment had the usual effect ; the whole of my fore-arm was affected with a cutaneous erysipelas, and there was disorder of the muscular nerves, accompanied with heat, redness, swelling, and pain. This attack lasted till Tuesday, and on Wednesday (October 7th) I was so far recovered that, following the same plan, I stung myself three times more also on the wrist. The attack of erysipelas this time was not nearly so severe ; but, as before, I felt a stinging sensation as far up as my shoulder, and I noticed that a lymphatic gland behind my ear had increased considerably in size, the poison being taken up by the lymphatic system. On Saturday (October 10th) I again treated myself to three stings, and the pain was considerably less, though the swelling was still extensive. At the end of the next week (October 17th) I had had 18 stings ; then I stung myself seven times more during the next week, and I reached the number of 32 on October 31st ; the course of the experiment having lasted very nearly four weeks. After the 20th sting there was very little swelling or pain, only a slight itching sensation, with a small amount of inflammation in the immediate neighbourhood of the part stung, which did not spread further ; and I stung myself on November 8th, without its having any effect on me."

Bees, when properly handled, seem in a great measure to know their masters. A nervous, fussy man, who attempts to disarrange them or their works will most certainly be attacked, whilst an adept in Bee-management, who will do what he has to do, calm, steady, and without fear, will mostly escape scot free. In removing frames with their attendant Bees, if care be taken not to jar them, or in any way to irritate the Bees unnecessarily, they scarcely seem to object at all. It is true that, like in our human hive, tempers vary, and some cantankerous, spiteful little fellow may make a dash at any part of us that is unprotected. If a person be attacked by Bees, no attempt should be made to retaliate; the assailed party should quickly retreat to the protection of a building or shady place, or, if none be near, lie down with his face to the ground. An angry Bee will seldom follow into the shade if the sun be shining. Violent winds seem often to make the Bees very angry, by blowing them about; but, as a rule, Bees do not volunteer an attack without cause. Langstroth, amongst his Bee-keepers' axioms, says: "Bees gorged with honey never volunteer an attack. Bees may always be made peaceable by inducing them to accept of liquid sweets. Bees, when frightened by smoke or by drumming on their hives, fill themselves with honey, and lose all disposition to sting unless they are hurt. Bees dislike any quick movement about their hives, especially any motion which *jars* their combs."

Many devices in the shape of Bee-dresses, some very ingenious, have been resorted to in order to protect the

Fig. 74.

wearer against being stung; but, as in many other things, the simplest is ofttimes best, and nothing more is requisite than a veil and gloves. An economical and very good veil is coarse black leno, costing fourpence per yard, made into a bottomless bag, 27 inches by 24 inches. In one end let be run half a yard of elastic, not too strong, which will complete the veil for use, as in figure 74, when on buttoning the coat up all is secure. The veil may be made at a cost of about sevenpence, and a duplicate or two kept handy for the use of friends, when inspecting one's Apiary, becomes very useful. For the hands, there is nothing better than good soft macintosh gloves, lined with some textile fabric, such as are used by photographers; but these require the addition of gauntlets (which may be made of calico or silk) to cover 2 or 3 inches of the coat cuffs, held in place by elastic run into their upper edge. Where the India-rubber gloves are not procurable, stout woollen or leather may be used, but are not so effectual; but an adept in Bee culture soon looks with contempt upon *gloves*, and I really think in my early Bee-keeping days when wearing gloves I got oftener stung on the hands, through carelessness in securely fastening my gauntlets, than I now do working with naked hands.

Thus equipped, the aspirant to Bee honours may bid defiance to his angry little friends, and in time confidence will be mutually established and, possibly, the gloves presented to a more unpractised hand; but even with the most experienced I should advise that the veil be kept in constant use, for accidents will happen, and stings about the eyes are never pleasant to any one. The Queen, although provided with a sting, never uses it, except in combat with another Queen; and it is scarcely necessary to say that Drones have no sting at all. Having been stung, the next consideration comes how to cure it, or at least reduce the effect to a minimum of discomfort. Many things are given as remedies, but I have no faith in any, except a good soaking in warm water in the manner most convenient. If the hands are stung, lay them in a basin of hot water, the longer time the better; if the face or other part, foment or poultice. When stung, remove the sting quickly, then, if possible, warm the pipe of a small key and press it over the puncture; a little drop of poison will, probably, appear, which remove; then apply a single drop of liquor potassæ, sal volatile, or chloroform, or rub well with sweet oil; either of these remedies will sometimes give relief, but they are neither specifics.

REMOVING BEES.

IT often becomes needful to remove Bees either from one garden to another, a new position in the same garden, or when they are sold or otherwise disposed of, perhaps the perils of a long journey will have to be endured. If the position of a hive be changed even a few feet, the Bees on returning home from their next flight get bewildered, and ofttimes lost. They do not, as one would think they would, readily discover their removed hive, and in their distress will often enter a neighbouring hive, when they are most inhospitably received. Care must therefore be taken that no needless removal should be made, and when it is necessary let the journey be made 2 or 3 feet at a time day by day. Should this not be convenient, let the stock be carried $1\frac{1}{2}$ or 2 miles away, and left there for a week or two, then it may be brought back and placed where desired with safety.

Hives with Bees in them, travelling for six hours or more, should always be carried mouth upwards, except frame hives, where the crown-board can be removed, and perforated zinc substituted. On a short journey, if the hive be not removed from the floor-board, it should be securely tied or nailed there, and perforated zinc be fixed before the entrance, and over the feed-hole at top. Swarms and stocks may be trusted for a few hours, covered with cheese-cloth or open towelling, but the Bees will gnaw through this if the journey be one of days. Newly-made combs will not stand much shaking, and these should only travel under the supervision of some careful persons; for, should the combs be shaken down, great destruction of Bees would ensue, and the owner would have considerable trouble in rectifying the mishap. When frame hives are sent away, two strips of wood, with pieces nailed to them to go between the frames to keep them apart, should be fastened over and under the frames. When Bees are to be removed by hand, they ride easily and safely on a light hand-barrow, which may be made of a couple of light poles, crossed by a few thick sticks. In hot weather it is not prudent to send a large swarm far in an otherwise unfurnished hive, the excitement causes the Bees to generate a great heat, often sufficient to suffocate them all.

PREPARATION OF WAX.

HAVING employed the Bees to extract every particle of honey from the combs, put the latter in a clean cloth, which sink in a copper of hot water, interposing a plate between the bundle and the bottom in order that the cloth may not burn; simmer over a clear fire, and as the wax melts, it will come to the top of the water, and may be taken off in a cake when cold. If preferred, the comb broken up small may be put into a saucepan of water, boiled, and when melted poured into a flannel bag also made hot and wet with boiling water; the melted wax will run through into a tub of water. In order to refine the wax the process will have to be repeated once or twice until the wax is pure. The wax may be bleached by running it into thin ribands and exposing these to the bleaching action of a grass plat for several days and nights, taking care the sun is not allowed to melt them.

ROBBING.

"HONESTY is the best policy," but Bees seem to think the contrary, and "might gives right" is a proverb more often acted upon by them. Should a hive become weak, and especially if Queenless, as soon as the state of affairs be discovered by a neighbouring strong family, a raid is organised. Poor Bees! gallantly do they defend their stores, and great the slaughter that ensues, but numerical strength is sure to conquer; when the assailed are fully assured that resistance is in vain, they act very wisely, and instead of fighting longer, turn to and help the invaders to carry off the stores, and in reward are received as new citizens in the free-booting hive. If a hive which is known to be weak be discovered in a state of unusual bustle and excitement, watch it narrowly; and if fighting be going on nearly close up the entrance for a few days, leaving room only for one or two Bees to pass at a time; a narrow door is more easily defended than a wide open gate. Should the assailants be very pertinacious, wet a piece of tow or moss with carbolic acid, and fasten it on the alighting board; the robbers will be too disgusted to pass, but the defenders will brave it. Fighting may often be ascribed to the Bee-keeper's carelessness in spilling honey or syrup round about a weak stock, which being discovered and appropriated by stronger Bees, they soon seek for more plunder in the same locality.   The Rev. Mr. Kleine says, robbers may be repelled by imparting to the hive some intensely powerful and unaccustomed odour.   He effects this by placing in it in the evening a small portion of musk, and on the following morning the Bees, if they have a healthy Queen, will boldly meet their assailants.   These are nonplussed by the unwonted odour; and if any of them enter the hive and carry off some of the coveted booty, on their return home, having a strange smell, they will be killed by their own household.   The best remedy against robbing is, however, to keep all stocks strong.

DRAINING HONEY FROM THE COMBS, AND HOW TO MAKE USE OF IT.

WHERE the honey-comb is pure and white, as is usual with combs built in supers, it is customary to send it to table whole and without bruising; but when the combs come from the main hive, where breeding has been going on, the honey must be drained and stored as clean and pure as possible.   Having a mass of such combs before us, it becomes advisable to sort them into qualities, all such as have Bee-bread or larvæ being put aside, then slice them transversely through the cells, and put them in a hair sieve or fine linen bag, leave them so two or three days, turning them over occasionally, and nearly all the honey will run out; do not press or crush them, and impurities will be avoided.   The strained honey should then be nicely skimmed, and the skimmings put with the strained and waste combs to make metheglin of; or should this not be desired, give the whole to the Bees in a bottle or super over the feeding-hole and they will carry down every particle of honey for their own subsistence or their master's necessities, should he determine to appropriate their stores. The filtering and refining will be done far better by the Bees than is possible by any human means. The strained honey should be poured into glass jars until they are *quite full*, then tightly tied over. Those honey-combs it is desired to reserve for table use should be neatly wrapped up in writing-paper and carefully put aside, the honey within the cells will be found clear and limpid many months afterwards. The pieces of combs, if any, containing brood should be stacked the same way upwards as they were built, and inserted in a small glass or super; this, if placed over the feeding-hole of another hive, will be taken possession of by the Bees from below, who will tend and rear the young, whose lives may be thus preserved.

Bees will sometimes gather honey from objectionable plants, of which laurel and ivy form examples; such honey, although not harmful to the Bees, may be intensely disagreeable to us. Where such is observed prudence dictates that it should be left for the Bees' own consumption.

HONEY—luscious honey—is generally a treat to our little ones for their breakfast, tea, or supper, in place of butter, and nice and wholesome it is too, as well as an agreeable change; but, unlike bread and butter, they soon tire of it, so it is only as a treat that it can be consumed in that way. To the buyer of 10 pounds or 20 pounds this does not matter, but where we keep our own Bees, and our little friends supply us with the delicious commodity by the hundredweight, then an important question arises—How to dispose of our honey?

Naturally the answer comes—Sell it. Very good, but first a customer must be found, and we do not all like to turn hawkers without a license ; so now I suggest we should take a lesson from our neighbours of the Continent, who have many ways of using honey to please all palates. Almost contemporaneous with our Crystal Palace Exhibition were held at Paris and Copenhagen gatherings of a similar character, and, in addition to most of the exhibits that were shown here, appeared a long list of eatables and drinkables made wholly or partly with honey, which would be very welcome on the tables of our own land. Taking the Paris catalogue, I see there were shown honey bread, spiced bread, fruits preserved in honey, jellies, sweetmeats, cakes, bonbons, pastiles, and chocolates ; whilst for eau de vie we need not leave old England, seeing it is to be made both from honey and wax! Then we have hydromel or metheglin, champagne, red and white wines, liqueurs, fruit syrups, vinegar, and fruit cordials. There is a pretty list of delicacies for our housewives to exercise their ingenuity and skill upon!

RECIPES. — METHEGLIN OR HONEY WINE.—When the comb has been drained of its honey, put it in a large vessel, then pour in sufficient lukewarm water to swim it nicely. Let it stand two days, stir occasionally, then strain it. Skim the scum from the liquor carefully, filter the sediment through a flannel bag, then boil one hour, and add three gallons :—two pounds raisins, one ounce of ground ginger, and seven or eight laurel leaves, then cool. Add a little brewer's yeast, let it stand part of a day, then barrel it, leaving the barrel open for two or three days ; bung it up, and let it remain untouched for six months, then bottle it. I daresay some who try their hands at making this honey drink will be anxious to taste before the expiration of the six months, but the longer it is kept the better it will be. If an egg will float on the liquor it will be about the right strength. Metheglin may, of course, be made from run-honey; but by soaking the combs in water we utilize the honey which would otherwise be lost. A little lump sugar put in each bottle will make it as fine as brandy.

ANOTHER.—Boil for one hour 20 pounds of honey in six gallons of water, and remove the scum as it rises; then add 3 ounces of hops and strain to cool. When milkwarm stir in a tablespoonful of yeast, and let it work 24 hours; skim off the yeast and put the liquor in a barrel; fill up daily as it works over, bung down, and bottle for 12 months, adding half a wineglassful of brandy to each bottle. The result is a very clear drinking vinus liquor.

HONEY CAKES.—Mix a quart of strained honey with half a pound of powdered white sugar, half a pound of fresh butter, and the juice of two oranges or lemons. Warm these ingredients slightly, just enough to soften the butter, and then stir the mixture very hard, adding a grated nutmeg. Mix in gradually two pounds or less of sifted flour, make it into a dough just stiff enough to roll out easily, and beat it well all over with a rolling-pin; then roll it out into a large sheet half an inch thick, cut it into round cakes with the top of a tumbler dipped frequently in flour, lay them in shallow tin pans slightly buttered, and bake them.

GERMAN HONEY-CAKES.—Take 3½ pounds of flour, 1½ pounds of honey, ½ a pound of sugar, ½ a pound of butter, grate half a nutmeg, ⅛ of an ounce of ginger, ¼ of an ounce of carbonate of soda; roll them, cut into small cakes, and bake in a hot oven.

AMERICAN HONEY-CAKE.—1 pound of honey, ½ a

pound of butter, 2 ounces of sugar, two eggs, one or two table-spoonfuls of milk or cream ; then to a quart of flour put two large tea-spoonfuls of baking-powder, and mix sufficient of this prepared flour to make the paste stiff as pound cake. Bake thin layers in tins, taking care not to over bake.

ANOTHER. — Soak three cups of dried apples over night, chip slightly, and simmer in a pint of honey for two hours; then add three quarters of a pint more honey, ¼ of a pound of sugar, ½ a pound of melted butter, three eggs, two tea-spoonfuls of baking-powder; flavour with cloves, cinnamon, powdered lemon, or orange-peel, or ginger. Mix all together with enough flour to make a stiff batter ; make into two cakes, and bake in a slow oven.

HONEY PUDDING.—Three pints of thinly-sliced apples, one pint of honey, one pint of maize-meal, small piece of butter, one tea-spoonful of carbonate of soda, the juice of two lemons and their grated rinds. Stir the dry soda into the honey ; then add the apples, melted butter, and a little salt ; now add the lemon-rind and juice, and at once stir in the flour. Bake one hour ; serve hot or cold with sauce.

HONEY VINEGAR is made as follows: "Put ½ a pound of honey to a quart of water, boiling hot ; mix well, and expose to the greatest heat of the sun without closing vessel containing it, but sufficiently so to keep out insects. In about six weeks this liquor becomes acid and changes to strong vinegar, and of *excellent* quality. The broken combs, after being drained, may be put in as much water as will float them, and well washed. The linens, also, and sieves which have been used for draining honey, may be rinsed in the same water, and with this make the vinegar; first boil and scum it before mixing it with the honey.

P

TO CLARIFY HONEY.—Melt the honey in a vessel standing in boiling water, strain, while hot, through flannel previously moistened with warm water.

Honey is prescribed by the medical council of Great Britain for use in the following pharmaceutical preparations, viz.: Confection of pepper ; confection of scammony ; confection of turpentine, honey and borax ; oxymel of squills, and simple oxymel.

THE END.

INDEX.

OPINIONS OF THE PRESS OF
THE FIRST EDITION.

———◆———

"It is profusely illustrated with engravings, which are almost always inserted for their utility. * * * * * There is an old saying that 'easy writing is hard reading,' but we will not say thus much of Mr. Hunter's book, which, taken as a whole, is perhaps the most generally useful of any now published in this country."
—*The Field.*

"In Mr. Hunter's book, there are many most interesting chapters on the History of Bees, their wonderful structure, ways, and habits, which the more they are looked into the more marvellous they appear. The profitable keeping of Bees is also fully gone into, and we are given many curious items respecting Bee-keeping in different countries."—*Weekly Times.*

"Mr. Hunter's instructions are simple and practical. He discusses fully the various forms of hives and the best method of treatment of Bees, urging strongly the advantage of large and well stocked hives. We can warmly recommend this little book to all who have a country garden, however small."—*Standard.*

"The author of this exceedingly useful manual is the Honorary Secretary of the British Beekeepers' Association, and as such, is thoroughly well up in the subject on which he writes so pleasantly, and concerning which, he has collected so much valuable information from other writers. The little volume is unpretentious and interesting, Mr. Hunter's object being to convey to his readers the fullest and most practical information on Bee-keeping, rather than to air his own knowledge, or to present himself as a very learned authority. He freely admits having given extracts from other authors, but it is only fair to a modest and delightful writer to say that his book is comprehensive, capitally arranged, and though hastily compiled, nowhere exhibits carelessness, either in style or subject matter."—*Public Opinion.*

"We honestly and conscientiously declare we have been both surprised and delighted with Mr. Hunter's work. Mr. Hunter deservedly merits the thanks of British Bee-keepers for his book, and we have long wondered why no one could be found sufficiently bold to take up the subject of Bee-keeping in an interesting and readable manner, so as to be attractive to the working Bee-man of this country, and at the same time to be within reach of their purse ; but we can now recommend them to secure the Manual of Bee-keeping, which meets a want long felt. Many chapters contain new thoughts and ideas, which we hope will act as a stimulus when placed under good influences, and bring forth abundant fruit.   Mr. Hunter has done his best to bring his knowledge up to date, and as he has most worthily completed his self-imposed task we trust he will be honoured, as he richly deserves to be, by a new edition soon being called for."—*Gardener's Chronicle.*

"We cordially recommend Mr. Hunter's neat and compact Manual of Bee-keeping; Mr. Hunter writes clearly and well."—*Science Gossip.*

"We are indebted to Mr. J. Hunter, Honorary Secretary of the British Bee-keepers' Association. His Manual of Bee-keeping, just published, is full to the very brim of choice and practical hints, fully up to the most advanced stages of Apiarian Science, and its perusal has afforded us so much pleasure that we have drawn somewhat largely from it for the benefit of our readers."—*Bee-keeper's Magazine (New York).*

" While practical lessons are invaluable, they by no means render the learner independent of good text books, and amongst these has appeared one by Mr. John Hunter, who, less ambitious to claim originality than to place in our hands a really useful manual, has pressed into his service, wherever practicable, the best authorities upon the specialties under consideration.   The only Palace show yet held, brought to the front so much that was both new and useful, that scientific Bee-culture rather advanced a leap than a step, and existing works were to some extent rendered obsolete.   The progress then made has been embodied in the book before us, which is, on the whole, for those who desire to be made *au courant* with the Apiculture of the day, the best we yet possess."—*The Country.*

"That Mr. Hunter's volume will soon reach to another edition we have no doubt, for it is a careful condensation, well arranged, of all the knowledge requisite for successful Bee-keeping.   The volume is illustrated by many well-executed woodcuts."—*Journal of Horticulture and Cottage Gardener, May 20th,* 1875.

CLAY AND TAYLOR, PRINTERS, BUNGAY.

CPSIA information can be obtained
at www.ICGtesting.com
Printed in the USA
LVHW051959151221
706292LV00002B/132